Road Maps to the Future

BY

BOHDAN HAWRYLYSHYN

PERGAMON PRESS

OXFORD · NEW YORK · TORONTO · SYDNEY · PARIS · FRANKFURT

U.K.	Pergamon Press Ltd., Headington Hill Hall, Oxford OX3 0BW, England
U.S.A.	Pergamon Press Inc., Maxwell House, Fairview Park, Elmsford, New York 10523, U.S.A.
CANADA	Pergamon of Canada, Suite 104, 150 Consumers Road, Willowdale, Ontario M2J 1P9, Canada
AUSTRALIA	Pergamon Press (Aust.) Pty. Ltd., P.O. Box 544, Potts Point, N.S.W. 2011, Australia
FRANCE	Pergamon Press SARL, 24 rue des Ecoles, 75240 Paris, Cedex 05, France
FEDERAL REPUBLIC OF GERMANY	Pergamon Press GmbH, 6242 Kronberg-Taunus, Hammerweg 6, Federal Republic of Germany

First edition 1980

British Library Cataloguing in Publication Data

Hawrylyshyn, Bohdan
   Road Maps to the Future
   1. Social evolution
   2. Social systems
   I. Title
   301.24   GN360   80-40690
ISBN 0-08-026115-9
ISBN 0-08-026114-0 Pbk

Printed in Great Britain by A. Wheaton & Co. Ltd, Exeter

Road Maps to the Future

Other Titles of Interest

GIARINI, O.
Dialogue on Wealth and Welfare

GIARINI, O. and LOUBERGE, H.
The Diminishing Returns of Technology: An Essay on the Crisis in Economic Growth

KING, A.
The State of the Planet

SAUVANT, K.
Changing Priorities on the International Agenda: The New International Economic Order

LASZLO, E.
The Inner Limits of Mankind: Heretical Reflections on Today's Values, Culture and Politics

BOTKIN, J. W., ELMANDJRA, M. and MALITZA M.
No Limits to Learning: Bridging the Human Gap

FELD, B. T.
A Voice Crying in the Wilderness: Essays on the Problems of Science and World Affairs

TECHNOLOGY IN SOCIETY
An International Journal

An interdisciplinary journal providing a forum for the discussion of the political, economic and cultural roles of technology in society, social forces that shape technological decisions and choices open to society in the use of technology.

HISTORY OF EUROPEAN IDEAS

Devoted to the study of the history of the cultural exchange between European nations and the influence of this exchange on the formation of ideas and the emergence of the concept of Europe.

Specimen copies provided on request.

Foreword

DR. BOHDAN HAWRYLYSHYN is one of the most distinguished scholars and advisers on business and economic affairs. I have had a close personal relationship with him as a fellow member of the Club of Rome and as a board member of the CEI (Centre d'Etudes Industrielles—International Management Institute, Geneva) of which he is the Director.

He has worked in several professions and therefore has varied learning experiences. He has a profound interest in the behaviour of individuals, the functioning and management of organizations and the effectiveness of different societies.

In the chapter on "Effectiveness of Societies—An Overview" there is a table which shows in a symbolic fashion the main prototype components of societal orders. I was much interested in it. According to his assertion in this book the main components of societal orders, on which nation-states are based, are a set of values, a form of governance and an economic system. Through objective analyses we need to gain an improved understanding of how different countries function. His method of analysing the state of nation-states is quite interesting.

We need to understand the different nation-states on their terms and not just in comparison to some standard reference country. This is particularly true of countries and economic systems which are not just emulations of superpowers like the U.S.A. and the Soviet Union. Both our ability and our desire to learn from different societal experiences have to increase.

He also advocates an 'ideological liberation' from 'doctrinaire nineteenth century ideologies' to a 'pragmatic ideology' that would have a universal appeal.

We must search for ways in which different societies can evolve, rather than become frozen in the molds of yesterday's beliefs, ideologies and problems. Unless they evolve, they become dysfunctional or have to be broken up through revolutionary upheavals.

Hopefully the direction of evolution of various societies will be such as to make them more compatible with each other, make it possible for them to be accommodated within a still very distant, but inevitable world order.

I hope that this book will contribute to the debate on road maps to the future and that this debate will be pursued by the people of many countries.

Dr. Saburo Okita

Preface

> In general people experience their present naively, as it were, without being able to form an estimate of its contents... They have first to put themselves at a distance from it... The present so to say must have become the past before it can yield points of vantage from which to judge the future.
>
> (SIGMUND FREUD)

I have lived for prolonged periods under five dissimilar political regimes, each with a different underlying ideology and each at a different stage of economic development. This, in some ways, is analogous to living through a series of historical periods in a country that undergoes a number of political, economic, and social evolutions or revolutions. Living through such experiments can provide some insights into the advantages and disadvantages of various systems, their assets and liabilities, their potentialities and limitations, their effectiveness or ineffectiveness.

I also went through various educational streams: engineering, management, economics. By chance more than by choice I have worked in several professions: as a labourer (lumberjack), technical researcher, manager, educator. These varied learning experiences, both formal and practical, allow one to "put oneself at some distance from the present", and gain some understanding of the explanatory power—and also of the limits—of various disciplines and of the relativity of things. Specifically, such experiences sharpen one's perception of the couplings between the key components of societal orders, i.e. values, political governance, and economic systems. These couplings then suggest why different societal orders emerged, what is their current state, and what paths they might follow in their future evolution.

The desire to share some of my perceptions and conclusions was triggered off mainly by the debate within and around the Club of Rome on "World Problematique". This debate improved our understanding of the growing gravity, complexity, and interrelatedness of problems that confront humanity at this rather crucial juncture. It sharpened the need to search for ways out of our predicaments, for ways that could lead us to a better tomorrow. I offer, in all humility, a partial analysis of where we are now, how we got there, and some suggestions on how we might evolve to more effective states.

This book is not so much a summary of literature as a distillation of observations and experiences shared with my colleagues and the many hundreds of executives and officials to whom I have lectured at the CEI in Geneva and in virtually all corners of the world. To them, as well as to many inspiring thinkers of all races, creeds, and professions whom I have the good fortune to know, goes my gratitude. Larry G. Franko read the manuscript; Maria Cattaui helped me edit it; Suzanne Gall typed it with rare enthusiasm.

BOHDAN HAWRYLYSHYN

Geneva
January 1980

Contents

Introduction

by Alexander King and Aurelio Peccei

OVER the last decade, a whole series of Reports made to The Club of Rome have attempted to throw light on various elements of the tangle of contemporary problems which we term the World Problematique and have stressed in particular the importance of the interactions between them, which are virtually ignored in much current policy-making which is done mainly on a sector by sector basis. The petroleum crises have dramatized and given a political reality to this approach, for who can deny that energy has major repercussions on the foreign policy of countries, on their balance of payments, on monetary affairs, the pattern of world investment, location of industry, the North/South problems, environmental considerations, national policies for science and technology and the life-styles of society?

Similar interactions are apparent with regard to many of the other more striking issues within the Problematique—for instance, the monstrous overkill accumulation of nuclear weapons, the consequences of the world population explosion, the generation of expectations which cannot be realized, and also many of the consequences of affluence.

With the recognition that the Problematique is a political reality and not merely a conceptual image, it becomes clear that an imperative for the survival of our societies, and possibly also of our species, is the need to learn how to manage the problems of scale, complexity, rapid change and uncertainty which are the characteristics of our contemporary world and about which we know very little. There is indeed a newfound realization, even in the biggest countries, of the interdependence of problems which much resembles the interdependence of nations. The stark question which now must be posed is whether the structures, policies and procedures of governments, the ideologies on which they operate, and in fact entire political systems, are capable of facing up to this reality.

Political systems and governmental structures as we now know them were constructed long ago when times were simpler; the main ideologies were shaped by history, much of which may well be irrelevant to the present situation. The capitalist system, for example, is based on the free operation of market forces; yet, with wages determined by negotiations which take little heed of productivity, with oil prices determined by political rather than economic considerations and, as is the case of quite a few countries, with unprofitable enterprises subsidized by the state, the market is no longer free; some adjustment has taken place, but not enough. Again, democracy has locked itself into the present and, to its peril, ignores or virtually ignores the future which existing trends are conjuring up; the four or five year cycles of parliamentary and presidential elections ensure that government and opposition parties concentrate on issues of immediate concern to the electorate, without looking further ahead. Furthermore all our political systems, East and West, have become encrusted in a bureaucracy which is devoted to the maintenance of the status quo.

Without criticism and pressure from outside, organizations seldom attempt to change policies and procedures which appear, or used, to work reasonably well; current methods are assumed to be the optimum or the only practical approach. In a benevolent environment alarm signals are rare, while threats seem too remote to keep organizations alert and free from complacency; lost opportunities are seldom admitted or, indeed, recognized. Problems are tackled sequentially, and errors arising from slightly inappropriate responses to slightly misunderstood challenges are brushed aside. Difficulties are regarded as temporary setbacks rather than consequences of inevitable trends. Yet, after decades of uninterrupted economic growth, the environment seems to be changing from benevolent to hostile and the old tricks no longer seem to work. The result is confusion. In many of the democracies the easy line is to blame the government in power and to vote in another— which does not do any better.

Beneath and beyond all this lies the most intractable political dogma of them all, the sanctity of national sovereignty. The nation-state, at least in today's generalized form, is a relatively recent phenomenon and is greatly cherished by those in power. Hardly an international conference begins without assertions of its sacrosanct nature. "The religion of contemporary society is sovereignty", said Toynbee, and he added "its Gods demand blood sacrifice". We do not have to search very far for the reason. Selfishness and egoism are universal attributes of all mankind and have served the race well during its evolution, through the mechanism of the survival of the fittest.

Individuals learned eventually to temper their selfishness through the acquisition of social characteristics—when this was indispensable for mutual security and for the organization of the means of existence and prosperity. The resulting social units—the village, the tribe, the city, and the nation-state, inevitably possess their own collective egoism which we refer to admiringly as patriotism, or sneeringly as chauvinism and jingoism. One sees this starkly in international nego- tiations with each nation's representatives bargaining on the basis of narrow, immediate self-interest, paying little heed to the general good or, indeed, even to the longer term interests of their own country. With the evolutionary trend towards larger units which the nation- state implies, there is a greater accumulation of power and hence the abuse of this power becomes much more dangerous than at the level of the village, tribe or city state. Today, with the emergence of a small number of super-powers supported by sophisticated military tech- nology, the danger to humanity is greater than at any time in man's history, and will remain so until a social cohesion is reached at the global level, as has already occurred at intermediate levels, to ensure the survival of the race and its institutions.

For the time being, though, even if, as Stanley Hoffman puts it, "the vessel of sovereignty is leaking", the nation-state is here to stay. On the other hand, for many of the new countries, recently decol- onized, whose populations consist of a somewhat artificial mixture of tribes brought together arbitrarily within boundaries drawn on the map by rival colonial powers a century ago, sovereignty, fragile though it may be, is one of the few cohesive forces extant and prob- ably must be maintained at all costs. We are thus unlikely to see a replacement of the present system of nation-states by any other kind of political architecture, such as a world government, in the near future. Indeed, the idea of a world government or a world federalistic approach is hardly advisable, since it is based on linear thinking stemming from present outmoded political theories and archaic structures.

What is encouraging, however, is that change and experiment are actually taking place, albeit unsystemically. Recognition of the essential interdependence of nations has led to many arrangements inside and outside the United Nations, to regulate issues of concern to several countries, ranging from the monetary field and international financial mechanisms to the law of the seas, the allocation of radio frequencies, the International Postal Union and a vast array of minor matters. Furthermore, the upsurge of a number of global problems, such as major threats to world environment and climate, the solution of which is beyond the capacity of even the largest nations, will inevitably lead to some elements of sovereignty being handed over to international control. In practice, there is thus a gradual but not inconsiderable functional loss of sovereignty.

All in all the need to make a determined start on the construction of a completely New World Order is undoubtedly great and long overdue. The new order must, of course, take into account the political and power realities of the present, but at the same time aim to move from current ideas of narrow and immediate self-interest towards a wider concept of common interest viewed in a long-term perspective. In preparing for it, we must be ready to question all contemporary ideologies, political dogmas and structural traditions.

It is against this background that we particularly welcome Bohdan Hawrylyshyn's exploratory book. Its title strikes exactly the right note as does the stress on the need for coexistence until the World Order emerges, and as a prerequisite to build it. He is particularly qualified by his background in many countries and by his experience as a pioneer in training for international management to present an objective and comprehensive view of world ideologies, systems and structures. His analysis of the variety of building blocks available to put together tomorrow's world is exceedingly clear and his national case studies well chosen to demonstrate the wealth of cultural strains which can be combined to make it viable and livable.

The method adopted to indicate possible paths towards the future is stimulating and leads the reader to realize how complex a task is that of bettering our quality of life and the human condition generally and how, at the same time, this depends almost exclusively on how intelligently we, generation after generation, are able to use the immense patrimony of knowledge, experience and means at our disposal.

Throughout the book this difficult job, namely, modern man's responsibility to shape the future of society, now on a planetary scale, is pleasingly presented in its many different aspects. Notable is the reference made to the European Community's experience at a moment when the regional approach to a new international order is receiving ever greater attention. What happens in Europe can in fact be highly instructive for those, in other parts of the world, who are confronted with the task of innovating political institutions but find the national environment too narrow and introvert a frame for so doing. Aggregation of power at a supranational level within regions and subregions will probably offer development opportunities which individual nations could never afford. At the same time, European experience shows that such a scheme can be successful only if it does not stifle the drive to greater self-assertion and self-determination which human groups possess even at local or district level.

For these reasons, The Club of Rome is very pleased to accept this as the latest of the series of reports it has requested, recognizing that it is the start of a new approach, indicating just a few of the milestones along what must be a long and challenging, but also a rewarding road. It is to be hoped that the book will provoke much discussion and even controversy and help to liberate us from outworn dogmas. The need for social and institutional innovation is indeed great and, if we all learn how to harness and channel the self-interest of nations towards the goal of wise, long-term common interest which, as these pages indicate, we are all being forced to accept, interdependence will become not a burden or a threat but an asset and a promise.

April 1980

CHAPTER 1

Effectiveness of Societies—
An Overview

Measures of Effectiveness

Societies—nations—vary greatly in their effectiveness over time and across boundaries. Economic performance can range from low productivity with great poverty to rapid economic growth with high prosperity, to stagnation or decline. Political conditions can vary externally from strength and influence to relative impotence, and internally from peaceful, smooth functioning of political institutions, with great personal and institutional freedoms and a high degree of voluntary acceptance of the governance system, to imposition of power, coercion, mass terror, civil strife, civil war, and revolution. Social health also varies and can change over time from congenial relations between people at work and leisure, with opportunities for creative, useful pursuits, cohesion, and commitment, to friction, tension, disintegration of social units, alienation, and high criminality.

The effectiveness of nations can be assessed according to economic, political, or social criteria. The three are obviously interlinked and cross-influence each other. Economic measures of effectiveness, being quantifiable, permit an easier evaluation and comparison of countries, even though there is no single, sufficiently meaningful index of economic performance.

Evaluations of political and social health, albeit more difficult, are made constantly in explicit studies and debates, manifested in feelings of satisfaction or discontent, expressed through attitudinal polls, strikes, or dissident movements.

It would be highly desirable to have a single composite measure by which we could assess the performance of nation-states, but such a measure does not exist and is not about to emerge. Assessments and comparisons, nevertheless, are made constantly, varying in rigour and objectivity. This methodological dilemma is dealt with in the Appendix, which gives a brief survey of present measures/proxy measures and indicators by which countries are being assessed.

Determinants of Effectiveness

But how do we explain the great variations in the "performance" of countries? What are the principal causes? There is a multiplicity of factors that condition behaviour and, thus, the effectiveness of societies. The linkages are shown schematically in Fig. 1.

The social health of society requires that there be some match between aspirations—expectations and accomplishments—realizations, dreams and reality, feelings of entitlement and their fulfilment. Because of the social nature of man, all of the above depend on the nature of relationships between people at various levels of societal structure. These in turn are moulded by beliefs—values as to what is right, desirable, justifiable.

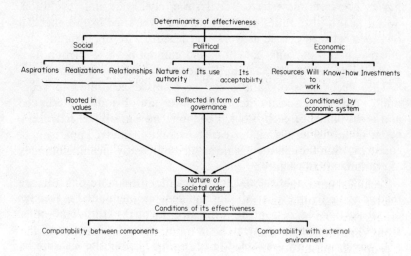

FIG. 1.

Political institutions function or malfunction depending on how power is aggregated, how it is used to direct resources and regulate relationships, whether it is seen as legitimate and just, forcibly imposed or voluntarily accepted. The above is determined by the nature of political governance.

A somewhat more detailed discussion of the preconditions of economic efficacy (shown in Fig. 1) will lead us to the conclusion that the nature of societal order is the key determinant of societal effectiveness.

1. *Resources* are not indispensable. Economic development is mostly man-made. Providence has helped and continues to help some societies by having bestowed on them rich natural resource endowments. Also, given the growing value of resources because of their diminishing stock, the greater the resource endowment the better the general economic prospects of a country. History shows that the availability of resources is not sufficient to trigger off or to sustain economic performance. Countries such as Japan and Switzerland have amply demonstrated that a proper combination of will and skill can make up for the absence of resources.

2. The *will* or motivation to work is influenced by religious beliefs; the perception of work as a necessity, a form of obligation towards family, social group, nation; as instrumental in satisfying material or social needs; or as the fulfilment of self or one's destiny.

3. Appropriate and constantly improving *know-how* is required in order to increase the fruit of hard effort. There are two categories of know-how:

   technical, which enables man to manipulate the forces of nature for his benefit; and
   organizational, which enables the creation and maintenance of effective organizations.

Technical know-how is more universally valid. Given a certain level of education and the will to learn, it can be more readily imported and absorbed. Socio-organizational know-how is culturally conditioned and needs to be in harmony with the beliefs of the people. It must, therefore, be mostly "home-grown".

4. For growth to be a sustainable process, the will and the know-how

have to be amplified by the proper equipment. There needs to be some "horsepower" behind every elbow and brain. This has to be accomplished through the process of *investment* in machinery, in physical and service infrastructures. The sources of funds for investment can be domestic, such as private savings or corporate profits, whatever their ownership, or external, such as foreign investments or aid.

For the will to work to be sustained, for know-how to be generated, disseminated, and implemented, and for adequate rates of investment to be maintained, the institutional framework, the *societal order*, has to be right. We can perhaps reformulate the determinants of effectiveness in the following way:

$$\text{Eff} = f\left(\frac{\text{resources}}{\text{population}} \text{ societal order, external environment}\right)$$

Components of Societal Order

Any societal order consists of three components: *values, political governance*, and *economic system.*

There are several distinctive sets of values, forms of governance, and economic systems; all of them have some intrinsic advantages and disadvantages. Some of them are more attractive from the humanistic point of view; some are appealing from the political, philosophical, or social point of view; some lead to better economic performance.

The main "prototype" components are as shown in Fig. 2.

I. VALUES

1. *Individualistic-competitive*

Each individual is unique. It is legitimate for each to be concerned with his own needs and aspirations and to seek self-assertion and self-fulfilment.

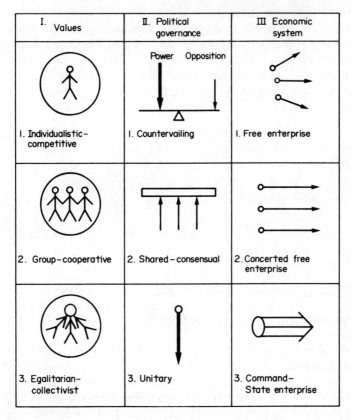

I. Values	II. Political governance	III Economic system
1. Individualistic- competitive	1. Countervailing	1. Free enterprise
2. Group-cooperative	2. Shared-consensual	2. Concerted free enterprise
3. Egalitarian- collectivist	3. Unitary	3. Command- State enterprise

FIG. 2.

2. *Group-cooperative*

A person is just one part of creation and one part of the societal fabric. Each should seek to play his proper role in it, voluntarily subordinate to higher purposes, to fulfil his obligations and his destiny through cooperative interaction with others.

3. *Egalitarian-collectivist*

People are born equal, and are an integral part of society. Each person should be able to draw on the common pool to satisfy his needs, but contribute to that common pool to the best of his abilities. Each finds his meaning and fulfilment through a communal type of existence in a conflict-free society.

II. POLITICAL GOVERNANCE

1. *Countervailing Powers*

This is representative government with one party in power and one or more in opposition, whose perceived purpose is to prevent abuse and improve the use of power, to "counter-balance". Freedoms are guaranteed by the separation of legislative, executive, and judicial powers.

2. *Shared-consensual Power*

Decisions are made by representatives of different sectors of the population, with varied orientations, partaking in the process and subsequently sharing the responsibility for the consequences.

3. *Unitary Power*

In this form of governance, power is concentrated at the top of the societal pyramid, with no official opposition or counterweight to it. This describes all dictatorships, from left to right, whatever their ideological justification.

III. ECONOMIC SYSTEMS

1. *Free Enterprise*

The key descriptors of this system are private property, profit maximization, and a free market, with government committed to ascertain the above within the rule of law, with predominantly adversarial relations between government, business, and labour.

2. Concerted Free Enterprise

This system has features similar to the above, except for more cooperative relations between government and business (and, in some countries, labour), enabling the creation of consensus about national objectives, priorities, and the ensuing harmonization of economic endeavours.

3. Command-State Enterprise

This system is characterized by state or "collective" property, output maximization, a regulated market, and the deterministic role of government in economic affairs, exercised through central planning and administrative allocation of resources.

Evolution of Societal Orders

Nation-states developed different forms of societal organization for a variety of reasons. There were strong beliefs about what was right and wrong, thus the kind of institutions that were required, as was the case in the United States in 1776. The colonial heritage was a major factor in India. A distinctive ideology, which prescribed the form of the political governance and economic system, was initially the main moulder of societal order in the Soviet Union.

Once established, the institutional features of societal orders tend to become "sanctified" and very difficult to change substantially, except through revolutions.

In the last few decades, many conditions have been changing rapidly. Empty spaces have diminished; resources have shrunk; interdependence within and between societies has increased. Some countries have gone rapidly through several stages of economic development, while others have gained or diminished in political stature. Needs, therefore, change, as do economic priorities and, as should, some values, political, and economic institutions in order to match better the new realities. Will the societal orders evolve along the desired directions to permit nation-states to continue to function effectively?

As we look at the symbolic representation of the components of societal orders, we can identify certain combinations with particular countries.

The *United States* can be described as having a predominantly individualistic-competitive set of values, a countervailing type of political governance, and a free enterprise economic system. The combination seems to be a natural fit. Until the recent past it was, and it facilitated great economic development, the spread and improvement of political liberties and rights, and led to a high degree of contentment of the population. However, now this societal order seems to be getting out of tune; there is a need for more restraint. Since its values do not evoke voluntary self-discipline and restraint, they have to be imposed through more legislation and bureaucracy.

As the country is about to move from the mass consumption stage* (in which the priority was to satisfy varied individual consumer needs) to the post-industrial society† (in which public consumption needs—such as education, health care, and clean environment—assume greater importance), the free market alone may not be an efficient and just allocator. Changes are needed in the societal order for the country to restore its effectiveness. Is it in the direction of more cooperative predisposition? Less adversarial conflictual orientation? More consensus seeking, power- and responsibility-sharing types of relationships and institutions with more voluntary harmonization of economic activities? These questions are examined in ch. 2.

Japan can be described as a country with a group-cooperative set of values, consensual though officially countervailing governance, and a concerted free enterprise economy in which the "economic quartet" (MITI, banks, trading houses, key firms) lead the rapidly paced economic march. The emergence of their particular values is understandable given the perceived nature of man as "being part of...", and their austere, limited, spaceship type of environment that has existed

---

*Rostow, W. W., *The Stages of Economic Growth: A Non-Communist Manifesto*, 2nd edition, Cambridge University Press, 1971.

†Bell, D. *The Coming of Post-industrial Society*, Heinemann, London, 1974.

for centuries. The consensual process in political and economic decision-making seems to flow naturally from their values.

The economic efficacy of this combination is evident enough: without much by way of resources, Japan became a growth champion. Is the above societal order "too economic" in its orientation? Is the psychic cost of voluntary subordination too high for some individuals? Can the cooperative, conflict-avoiding, consensus-seeking predisposition, which seems to function well at the work-group, company, and even national levels, be applied externally? Can the Japanese transcend their national interests to contribute to the construction of an effective world order?

The *Soviet Union* started with a blueprint for a societal order based on egalitarian-collectivist values, a unitary power system (dictatorship of the proletariat), and a command-state enterprise economic system. Differences between the blueprint and actual practices exist, since concessions have been made and expedients are being used during the so-called "transient socialist phase" on the road to communism. Some individualistic-competitive values have survived the revolution and have been amplified in order to create the material base for affluence—the necessary condition for the introduction of communism. The unitary power system has been preserved with the Communist Party "incarnating" the will of the proletariat. The political and social costs of this type of governance seem very high to many people.

The command, centrally planned economy accelerated the pace during the early industrialization or take-off stages of economic development. But, as the economy is approaching the mass consumption stage, many different points are required at which economic decisions can be made and initiatives undertaken in order to satisfy better the growing and diversifying needs of the population.

Can the Soviet societal order evolve? Can genuine egalitarian-collectivist values be nurtured? Can the monolithic power be spread to different levels of the societal hierarchy, since the state should ultimately "wither away"? Can the economic system be decentralized without prior decentralization of political power? Can, in other words, the societal order be reshaped to match the original design, or is a new blueprint needed?

China, after humiliating foreign interventions and a protracted, painful civil war, has been reshaping fundamentally its societal order since 1949. The leadership opted for a design consisting of egalitarian-collectivist values, unitary power, and command-state enterprise. Great efforts were exerted to inculcate new values in order for the young institutions to function. The costly cultural revolution was undertaken to "purify the souls". Priority is now given to "the four modernizations". Will this lead to the resuscitation of individualistic-competitive drives and motives? Will a trade-off be made between egalitarian-collectivist values and technological progress? If so, might the political governance and economic system get out of tune with such new values?

The dominant factors affecting mankind over the next two decades are discernible: growing population, shrinking resources, twilight of the "petroleum civilization", rapid urbanization, and massive unemployment in the Third World, increasing education, expanding aspirations, growing interdependence, yet also mutual total destructive capacity, hence the imperative for different societies to coexist in reasonable peace.

What kind of societal orders can best cope with the above conditions? Is it the individualistic, countervailing powers, free enterprise type? Is it the orders based on collectivist values, unitary powers, and command economies? Or might it be the societies with group-cooperative values, shared power, and concerted free enterprise that can confront with least difficulty the world of tomorrow? Is this type of societal order the precursor of at least a phase of evolution that many societies may have to go through as they approach a distant world order?

Some societal orders have occurred as accidents of history. Some are firmly rooted in particular ideologies that postulate that there is only one right way of organizing a society, which is valid for all countries and all times. We are now approaching, though, a better understanding of how the three components of societal orders interact and what conditions their effectiveness. With such improved knowledge, we should be able to take ourselves off our various ideological hooks, do some more societal design, and enable the type of political leaders to emerge who could mobilize their respective societies to change some values, restructure political and economic institutions, without going through political convulsions. We may, then, be able to build better bridges between different societies to help Mother Earth carry us into the future.

The above summary reflections are analysed in greater depth in the next chapters so as to be able to answer the questions raised. In addition to those already mentioned, a few more of the key countries are added to cover a broader spectrum of societies.

CHAPTER 2

The State of Nation-States

MUCH of the world's economic activity is generated, most of the military power is maintained, and political influence exercised by a few northern hemisphere, industrialized countries such as the United States, the Soviet Union, Japan, and states of Western Europe taken together. China fits into this category not by its level of development, but by its sheer numbers and the degree to which its population seems mobilizable for economic, political, or military objectives.

The rest of the world consists of a multitude of nations, many recently emerged. They vary in size from continental to postage stamp, in resource endowments from floating on petroleum to having nothing; in future potential they range from the new growth champions (South Korea) to those destined to continue a long march of relative misery (Chad). This so-called Third World, through permanent or temporary coalitions, exercises an increasing political influence through various forums. It will help shape the economic and political world of the future, but only some of its members will break through to individual significance before the end of this millennium.

This chapter attempts a politico-economic guided tour through all the countries or regions mentioned in the first category and a few selected ones in the second. The choice of countries is neither definitive nor accidental. The sample should be sufficient to indicate ways in which countries with radically different societal orders could evolve. The commentary will be in the form of a brief historical review and audit of strengths and weaknesses, assets and liabilities, as well as an analysis of compatibilities and mismatches in their societal orders. Finally, some indications will be given of the roads that could lead them to better futures.

THE UNITED STATES

1. Its Recent Past

For slightly over two decades the USA occupied a position of absolute pre-eminence in the world. This was solidly based on three pillars of strength:

—the world's biggest economy;
—the most potent military arsenal;
—the high morale of its people and their faith in the country's great destiny.

During the past decade, the country's position on the world stage has been scaled down. This is due to partial erosion of the above three pillars of strength. The economy, while undisputedly still the biggest, no longer appears to be the most effective. The USA has not produced the highest rates of growth of GNP, its ranking on GNP per capita has slipped and its currency has significantly weakened. The export performance is sluggish, the absolute dominance of its firms among the world's biggest multinationals has been significantly reduced, and the flow of foreign investments has partially reversed. Finally, in sharp contrast to the aggregate wealth, there are some millions of really poor people in the USA—a situation that has been relegated to the past in a number of smaller, weaker Western European countries.

The USA's military power has increased its overkill capacity and diminished its utility as an instrument for exercising political influence. The introduction of atomic weapons has, in a sense, sterilized military power, particularly in a country like the USA. This has happened for two reasons. First, the destructive power of the existing atomic arsenals is such that the cost in physical and human terms of any all-out war would be enormous—beyond the recovery capacity of even the potential winner of such a conflict. The cost–benefit analysis of undertaking such a war looks totally negative. Secondly, given the fairly humanitarian values of the American society and its political system, it does not appear conceivable that the USA would start an atomic war. The example of the Vietnam war, where the choice may have been between atomic weapons or defeat, is very telling. The only thing that the atomic arsenal does is to provide a defensive deterrent and an umbrella over Europe and Japan. At quite some cost, more and more warheads continue to be sunk into the silos, more numbers added to the inventory. Yet the ability of the USA to have its way in the world by flexing its military muscle has shrunk.

The political strength of the USA was backed by the greatest economy and military arsenal, but in addition it had its own intrinsic source: high political morale, which provided the will to play a leadership role. This morale was rooted in the profound conviction of the majority of Americans that they had the best country, the most efficient economy, the best political institutions, the freest society—all making their country a model for others to emulate. The past successes of the USA—the victory in the Second World War, the quick recovery after the war, the success of the Marshall Plan, and the feeling that the "American dream" was nearly fulfilled and could be exported—generated the will to manage as much of the world as would be willing to be managed, for the good of that world and not just for the good of America.

This high morale, which makes it easy to mobilize human energies, has been weakening, belief in the country's destiny has deteriorated, and, thus, the will and ability to "help the world get on the right track" is impeded. There are a number of converging causes: first, the Vietnam war, both the questionable wisdom of getting into it and the humiliation of getting out of it defeated. Secondly, there is the continued Soviet challenge. How can a country with a "wrong" political and economic system produce some real scientific accomplishments and build up such military power? Thirdly, there is the petroleum crisis. The vulnerable situation of this critical supply was made even more bitter to digest by the feeling of relative impotence to counteract the arbitrary moves of the "lesser" petroleum-producing countries. An additional factor is the unconditional support of Israel. While fully understandable because of profound sympathy for the past suffering of the Jews, the strength of their political lobby, and a genuine admiration for Israel as a democratic country created out of desert, this total commitment has been a serious obstacle in the way of a "natural alliance" between the USA and its main oil suppliers.

Some purely domestic developments have added to the loss of morale. The "melting pot" concept has not fully succeeded in fusing different ethnic groups into a homogeneous national amalgam; ethnic and racial revivals put some strains on the society. Watergate, even if finally well handled, was a great shock. The near bankruptcies of some big cities was another. The continued disparity between the rich and the very poor, the growing amount of legislation and regulations, the evident loss of some of the proverbial American efficiency all raise the question: Do we really have an ideal societal order that could be used as a model by the rest of the world?

The evidence of this loss of faith and morale is ample, particularly in a number of attitudinal surveys* showing an almost dramatic reduction in the confidence that the people have in their government, political leaders, big corporations, and other institutions.

2. Its Present State

One can establish a "balance sheet" of the assets and liabilities of the USA by refering to the "formula" of societal effectiveness as described earlier:

$$\text{Eff} = f\left[\frac{\text{resources}}{\text{population}} +/\text{or} \left(\begin{array}{c} \text{societal order, will,} \\ \text{know-how, investment} \end{array} \right) + \text{ext. world} \right]$$

2.1. ASSETS

—Large territory, broad range of natural endowments.
—Productive agriculture, which will continue to generate big surpluses in a food-hungry world. This is due to the natural fertility of the abundant land, amplified by the high motivation of owner-farmers, combined with the appropriate know-how, machinery, and infrastructuree.
—The will or motivation to work productively is still widespread;

*Yankelovich, D., The status of resentment in America. *Social Research*. vol. 42 (4). Winter 1975.

much of the motivation is based on material or other personal rewards.

—Know-how of the avant-garde type in all fields of technology and management; the ability to create original scientific knowledge, convert it into useful innovations in the form of processess, products or procedures; the ability to structure and manage organizations of varied size and complexity; very extensive and diverse educational system; some carry-over of former pragmatism.

—The industrial base, created by a century of high rates of investment, is very broad and diverse, as is the physical infrastructure of transportation and communication.

—The institutional framework, by continuing to reward private initiative, allowing different political interests to surface, and letting the free market do much of the allocation of resources, is still conducive to political and economic dynamism.

—To the external world, the USA is still a power to be reckoned with—admired by some, needed by others.

2.2. LIABILITIES

—The resource base is inadequate (energy, many minerals), given current and projected consumption levels and patterns.

—The will to work hard and productively is dissipating. Some take affluence for granted; the "Protestant" religious motivation seems weaker; strictly material rewards and the accompanying rat-race are less appealing to some (e.g. the voluntary simplicity movement); the humanistic motive, with work seen as an opportunity for self-expression or service, is not strong enough.

—Know-how of the socio-political kind—on how to manage racial problems, cities, health care, or economic inequities—seems inadequate. Given the weight of the country's experience, its size, and its past successes, it is difficult for the USA to learn from the positive experiences of other countries in fields such as government, business, and labour relations.

—Investment rates are low. They seem insufficient and not well enough directed to prevent the loss of competitiveness in a number of sectors and to prepare a smooth transition from a petroleum to a nuclear, solar, or other industrial civilization.

The most serious liabilities seem to be on the institutional front, with components of the societal order appearing out of harmony with each other and the physical environment. The present system is based on individualistic-competitive values, a countervailing-powers form of governance (representative democracy with checks and balances) and a free enterprise economy, represented symbolically in Fig. 3.

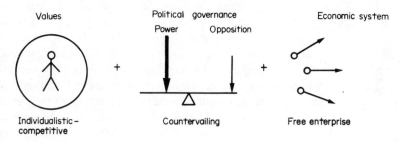

FIG. 3.

The above societal order was obviously highly effective for most of America's past history, particularly during the so-called "cowboy economy" era.* Until recent decades, the USA was a country with enormous resources, relatively sparse population, and virtually open frontiers. Dominant values emphasized rugged individualism, initiative, self-assertiveness, and even self-seeking, and provided a great stimulus for the domestication of the continent. The more each person undertook, reached out for, and accomplished, the better it was for all.

The free enterprise system, based on private corporations, unfolded its wings just as America was ready for the next industrial pioneering phase—building big factories, producing on a large scale, using rapidly developing technology. Again, the more individual companies undertook and the more sharply they competed, the better it seemed for the country. The labour movement, as it developed, focused on

*Boulding, K., Economics of the spaceship earth, *Environmental Quality in a Growing Economy: Essays from the 1966 RFF Forum*, Johns Hopkins Press, 1968.

getting a greater share of the pie, leaving the responsibility for baking it in the hands of management. A countervailing type of governance, with its checks and balances, seemed a natural institutional capstone for a country with an assertive, expansionist, dynamic population. It allowed a lot of energy to be applied in all directions, resulting in innovation and progress, yet prevented gross excesses. The generally adversarial relations between government, business, and labour seemed more of an incitement to out-perform the others, rather than a brake on effort.

In the last two decades the frontiers began to close in. The attractive spaces have been occupied, some resources have begun to look finite, and mother nature has begun to groan under the excessively active, potent, and occasionally reckless population. The elbow room has gone. Shrinking ecological space, combined with the mobility and drive of the population, created congestions and demanded restraints, such as more considerate treatment of the environment, more responsible behaviour of organizations and individuals towards each other, curtailment of certain appetites, and delineation of the outer limits of self-assertion.

The most effective response to the change from cowboy economy to spaceship earth would be to shift some beliefs and behaviour toward more self-control, voluntary discipline, and cooperative predisposition. But such changes take time. The main response instead has been to turn to the law. Since the USA is a country of "rule by law, not by man", an instinctive turning towards legislative means is understandable.

To impose the necessary constraints on individuals, corporations, and organizations, laws have been passed, agencies created to police them, and new "rules of the game" and limits constantly tested through litigation. The result is a near orgy of legislation–regulation–litigation. The existence in the USA of 600,000 lawyers is significant: on a per-capita basis, this is about three times more than in most Western European countries and ten times more than in Japan. If it is not the cause, then it is at least the consequence of the above legislative binge. The result is a disproportionate amount of energy absorbed by activities that do not contribute to the stock of goods, services, satisfaction, serenity, nor to economic competitiveness with other countries, which can rely more on self-discipline and self-control than on legislatively and, thus, bureaucratically imposed constraints.

On the economic front, the priorities are shifting also. Most of the needs for individual consumer goods (e.g. appliances) can now be satisfied. Public needs in areas such as quality education, health care, and pleasant environment are coming to the forefront. The genuinely free market may not be able to do a good job in allocating resources to such needs. This evokes more government intervention.

The political institutions are strained. A great deal of power is concentrated in the hands of the president, yet his burdens appear to be weightier than his powers. He has final responsibility for the management of a very complex country, for relations with the rest of the world, and for maintaining a happy balance of magnanimity and national self-interest, while being constrained by the Constitution and Congress and inhibited by institutionalized pulls and pushes in all directions. This seems to require a president who is a superman—but there is no place for a superman in a democracy. The president is now frequently "brought down to earth" and cut down to size, with the hope that the next one will provide the required "leadership".

The country's position *vis-à-vis* the external world is weakening. The USA is less of a reference model than it was two decades ago, be it in the fields of politics, economics, technology, or management. This results from a cumulative effect of significant progress on some social and political fronts in certain European countries and the remarkable economic performance of some Asian countries (Japan, South Korea), much of it initially triggered off by American help and subsequently fed on American technical know-how.

On balance, the liabilities of the USA seem to outweigh its assets. Some further loss of position relative to the rest of the world as a whole (not to a particular country) is therefore understandable and highly probable. The main cause lies in the fairly sudden occurrence of a mismatch between the three components of the societal order: values, political governance, and economic system. They are no longer in tune with each other nor with the new internal and external realities. They appear to need major restructuring and not just a minor overhaul.

3. Future Directions

The above three components of the societal order should be better harmonized and synchronized if the country's great physical and human potential is to be harnessed for serving the population's economic objectives, its political aspirations, and social needs. Values should probably change first and most. Political institutions should then be altered. The free enterprise economic system could then function better without fundamental changes.

3.1. VALUES

The main thrust, the main direction of changes in values should be from individualistic/self-centred/competitive to community conscious/cooperative. Represented symbolically the changes might be as Fig. 4 shows.

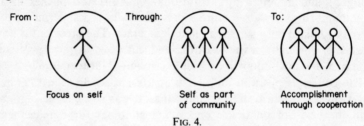

From :   Through: To :

Focus on self   Self as part   Accomplishment
of community   through cooperation

FIG. 4.

As already mentioned, the first set of values was highly effective in a "cowboy" and even industrial pioneering environment; the last seems more suitable for the approaching "spaceship earth" environment.

Schematically, and with sharpened contrast for illustration, the two sets of values can be represented as shown in Table 1.

To prevent further deterioration and to bring about necessary institutional changes and renewal, some such changes in values should occur within a couple of decades. Is this conceivable?

The answer seems quite positive for several reasons:

(a) Many of the "new" values have roots and multiple manifestations in the American past. Christianity not only proclaims that

TABLE 1

Individualistic-competitive	Community-conscious, group-cooperative
Primacy of individual	Individual is part of community
Man is a unique creation above and master of nature	Man is part of creation— seeking symbiosis with nature
Can legitimately focus on own needs, aspirations	Has some needs and recognizes those of others
Seeks self-fulfilment through:	Seeks fulfilment through:
self-assertion	use of talents
self-exteriorization	with constraint
self-reliance	self-discipline
individualistic competitive behaviour	sense of duty
to achieve success	in a cooperative
within limits of law,	mode of behaviour,
while showing tolerance,	to accomplish with
compassion for others	benefit to self and others,
	as directed by moral codes, social conventions

man was made in the image of God, but also prescribes: "Do unto others as you want others to do unto you". This commandment points in the desired direction and can be resuscitated. Spontaneous mutual help was as much a part of the pioneering past as was "shooting it out". Thrift and self-discipline were often conditions of survival. Such past virtues have been pushed a bit into the background, but may not have fully atrophied. They could be resurrected.

(b) Pragmatism was a dominant trait of the American people in the past. Pragmatism means recognizing reality and changing it if you can, adapting to it if you cannot. Recent changes in realities have been rather dramatic and, therefore, likely to evoke pragmatic response. The physical environment, which used to evoke expansionist, aggressive behaviour, has shrunk from virgin lands to expensive lots, with only the sea and space as new commons. The need for some self-restraint, sharing, and cooperation is patently evident. The world outside the USA has also changed: from a world literally saved by the Americans, through a world divided into two influence zones (American and Soviet), to a pluralistic world with multiple sources of power and influence. Learning how to contribute to the construction of a new world order by accommodating to its pluralistic nature, learning how to share power, and cooperate with different people on their terms, are the new conditions for playing a significant and constructive role on the future world stage.

(c) American society is of a pluralistic nature. One of the positive consequences of the fact that the "melting pot" process was only partly successful is that American society, and therefore its values, are not fully homogeneous. The "typical" values presented earlier are the dominant ones rather than the only ones. One finds in the USA adherents to very different philosophies and values and manifestations of very different behaviours. One finds, for instance, that some Japanese subsidiaries are operating successfully in the USA using the Japanese management style, which is rooted in the group-cooperative type of values. This means that American society is permeable to new ideas; it can change its dominant beliefs without cataclysmic events.

(d) The search for new values is already on: from the intellectual inquiries* of a somewhat earlier period, to more current review through economic optics,† to re-examination of changing values through management optics,‡ and, finally, to the grass-roots manifestations of new life styles with well-articulated values.§ In fact, some basic premises underlying voluntary (as opposed to imposed) simplicity are worth citing.‖

The right-hand side of Table 2 shows the intermediary, transition type of values that are being searched for within the American society.

Given the right antecedents in its own cultural heritage, the tradition of pragmatism for "finding things that work", the new environment, which makes old values dysfunctional, the pluralistic nature of American society and the evidence of a fairly broad search for new beliefs, one can conclude that a substantial reorientation of values is not only possible, but highly probable within the next few decades.

*Bell, D., *The End of Ideology*, Free Press, New York, 1962.

†Boulding, *op. cit.*

‡Lodge, G. C., Top priority: renovating our ideology, *Harvard Business Review*, September–October 1970.

§Elgin, D. and Mitchell, A., Voluntary simplicity (3), *The Co-Evolution Quarterly*, Summer 1977.

‖*Ibid.*, p. 15.

TABLE 2

Emphasis on industrial world view	Emphasis on voluntary simplicity world view
Values premises:	Value premises:
Material growth	Material sufficiency coupled with psycho-spiritual growth
Man over nature	People within nature
Competitive self-interest	Enlightened self-interest
Rugged individualism	Cooperative individualism
Rationalism	Rational and intuitive

3.2. POLITICAL GOVERNANCE

As new values start taking firmer roots, the political institutions can be reshaped to stay in harmony with them. The main direction of changes should be to shift from a fairly centralized, though nominally federal, countervailing-powers form of governance, through a more decentralized and diversified exercise of power, to shared power, a direct democracy model. Symbolically, this can be represented as shown in Fig. 5.

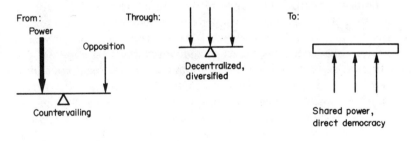

FIG. 5.

The main design features of the new system might be the following:

(a) *Decentralization* of decision-making powers to the state, county, or even local community level. Only foreign relations (both political

and economic), defence, some coordination in the fields of communication, transportation, and the general legal framework should
remain federal prerogatives. Education, health, welfare, and most
economic matters would be dealt with by authorities closer to the
people.

(b) Along with decentralization, more *direct democracy* should be
introduced: decisions having a major impact on the population
would be made by the relevant electorate through direct voting
on an all-country, state, county, or community level. Initiatives and
referenda would be used at various levels to force a general
vote on new issues or proposals, or to repeal laws made by elected
representative bodies. Decentralization and direct democracy could
be designed so as to give the now-educated, politically aspiring population both the opportunity to participate directly in the making of
political decisions and the responsibility of living with the consequences of these decisions. This should reduce the present alienation
from political institutions and increase the loyalty and commitment
to them.

(c) With a greater direct political involvement of the citizenry,
more *diversification* of organized political groupings would probably
take place. The heterogeneity of the American nation would be more
readily accepted as a permanent reality rather than a transient
phenomenon that could evaporate through a "melting pot" process.
The two national parties now differ more in emphasis and personali-
ties than in political programmes. New parties, possibly grouping
consumerists, ecologists, labour, and some ethnic groups, might
emerge, at least at regional levels, to offer sharper alternatives and to
press for priorities as they perceive them.

(d) The most important, even if not the most probable, shift should
be to *coalition type of governing bodies* at all levels, i.e. executive
organs consisting of representatives from various political groupings
in proportion to the votes drawn. Such executives would be elected
by the respective legislative bodies and thus be mandated by them
rather than by the parties. At the federal level this would mean a
cabinet elected by the vote of both houses in proportion to the political representation in the houses. The president would be similarly
elected and his main task would be to preside over the cabinet, which

would function in a collegial fashion, with each member having rather broad powers within his portfolio.

The access to power should be through a gradual, upward cascading process: people would serve first at local and regional levels, and only then be elected to national office. Thus, having demonstrated their competence, integrity, and dedication at various levels of governance, they could accede to the top, elected by those close to them who are able to judge them. This would reduce greatly patronage and potential abuses of power by having "filters" through which would pass those who wish to serve their community, state, or nation, rather than those who hunger for power or its spoils, be they only in the form of royalties for sensational memoirs.

The processs would lower the rate of turnover in top executive posts as well as slow down some of the decision-making. And it would also reduce the probability that someone without much national or international experience could short-circuit the whole system with a good electoral campaign and then be unable to cope with the tasks. The system would be dampened: less pre-electoral excitement, but fewer post-electoral deceptions; less sudden changes, but greater stability and predictability.

The above changes seem rather fundamental. Are they feasible? They do appear possible both for some negative and some positive reasons:

(a) There is serious *dissatisfaction* in many sectors of the American population with the functioning of the present political governance of the country. Much of the blame is still put on individuals involved, but some is beginning to focus on the flaws in the present institutional arrangements.

(b) Since the USA has been losing a certain amount of its world pre-eminence, it will be easier for many of its people to look at and *learn* from institutional alternatives as tested in *other societies*. Some of the features described above exist and function reasonably well in a couple of West European countries.

(c) One of the traits of Americans as a nation is the *ability to generate a new trend* and create a big momentum behind it once a clear purpose is identified and understood. The prospect of "putting the nation back on the tracks" and then being able again to show some other nations the way to the future, might be appealing enough to generate sufficient consensus behind the need for constitutional and institutional reforms.

(d) The existence of *bi-partisan committees* in Congress, or the reaching out beyond the party faithful in the formation of cabinets, show the capacity within that society to transcend narrow interests.

(e) The fact that *Democrats and Republicans differ so little* in their programmes (a bit more or a bit less pro business or welfare or minority rights) with no fundamental ideological clashes, should make it possible for them to start sharing power and responsibility provided this will not be perceived as abandonment of democracy and reduction of freedoms, but rather as an up-grading of democracy and an extension of freedoms to and involvement of a greater portion of the population.

(f) Finally, the above changes assume that *values would have already shifted* towards more cooperation, sharing, and greater voluntary integration into the societal fabric.

3.3. ECONOMIC SYSTEM

If values and political governance were to evolve in the directions indicated, no fundamental changes would need to take place in the economic system. The changes would be from an unbridled free enterprise economy to a concerted free enterprise system. Symbolically, the evolution would be shown as in Fig. 6.

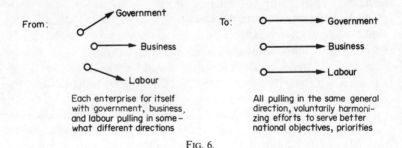

From:

Government
Business
Labour

Each enterprise for itself with government, business, and labour pulling in somewhat different directions

To:

Government
Business
Labour

All pulling in the same general direction, voluntarily harmonizing efforts to serve better national objectives, priorities

Fig. 6.

The main challenges for economic reforms in the USA would be to:

(a) Preserve the advantages of private initiative, such as motivation, drive, and the innovations stemming from it.

(b) Reduce economic wastages and abuses, such as high energy and other resource-intensive modes of production, overcapacities, underutilization, excessive stimulation of trite or even harmful wants, reckless domestic competition.

(c) Increase the flow of resources to communal consumption needs, such as good education, health care, public transportation, clean environment, healthy communities.

The main features of the free enterprise system would thus be retained, but the roles and manifestations would be altered:

(a) Maximization of profits would not be acceptable as the sole purpose and justification of any enterprise. Profit, however, would be legitimate and required as an indicator of surplus of outputs over inputs of any enterprise, thus an indicator of economic uses of resources, an indispensable precondition for viability and development of an enterprise and the benefits associated with it (useful goods or services, employment, taxes to finance public needs, etc.).

(b) Private property could be retained for all industrial and service enterprises except in the fields of education, some parts of communication, health care, public transportation and other services in which lack of private initiative, lack of profit prospects, or undue risks might deprive society of satisfaction of more communal needs.

(c) A free market could remain the main allocator of most resources, and particularly of individual consumer goods. The idea that competitiveness is now determined mostly in international markets rather than within domestic boundaries would be fully accepted and the open economy maintained. Firms would internalize more responsibilities and constraints, and moderate their behaviour towards others through self-imposed explicit statements of their missions, objectives, policies, or codes of ethics, as is already becoming a trend.

(d) The role of government would change. There would be less emphasis on controls through legislation and regulations, more on harmonization of objectives through indicative forecasting, less on antitrust but more on maintenance of productivity and restructuring of industrial sectors. There would be a substantial shift from adversarial to more cooperative relations between government, business, labour, and other societal leaders for setting of national priorities and objectives. Companies and other organizations would see themselves as instruments for serving societal needs.

Are these modifications of the free enterprise system, in which firms subordinate themselves more readily to societal needs, behave responsibly and concert their future plans, desirable and feasible?

An affirmative answer can be supported by the following:

(a) A shift to a command economy with central planning and administered markets does not appear overly attractive and most Americans are allergic to it. The experience of countries with such a system shows that it is too constraining as they reach more advanced stages of economic development. A number of socialist countries are trying to evolve out of it by reinstating profitability as a performance indicator, giving greater autonomy to business organizations and allowing determination of some prices by free markets.*

(b) The nationalization route, without shifting to a fully planned economy (i.e. by keeping freedom of markets), does not have a good record either. It is too easy a political expedient for preservation of existing industries and jobs. This is done by skimming off the efficient to keep alive the inefficient, thus reducing the developmental and job-creating capacity of the efficient firms and sectors.

(c) The impressive example of recent economic performance champions like Japan and South Korea show the power of essentially liberal economies with cooperative government–business relations.

(d) The continued good performance of West Germany shows that a "partnership" relation between management and labour is feasible and, in fact, a contributing factor to economic efficacy and political stability.

*Glinski, B., *System of Central Management of the Socialist Economy and Its Evolution*, Oeconomica Polona, 1979, no. 1, pp. 45–61.

(e) The search for new modes of interaction between business and government is on in the USA. The creation of the Business Round-table is but one example of this search.

(f) Significant steps are already underway in the direction of self-control, such as better representativeness of boards and their greater responsibility. Corporations have caught the "fever" of social responsibility and seek exterior manifestations through policy statements, management audits, and codes. Such public pronouncements of good intentions can be infectious and tend to grow into an obligation to act as one has promised.

Such are some of the roads that the USA could travel during the next few decades. They could lead to the resurrection of some of America's greatness, to convergence with similar developments in other societies, and, thus, to a better synchronization and more effective relationship with the rest of the world. These steps constitute the preparatory moves towards a still distant but inevitable world order.

THE SOVIET UNION

1. Its Recent Past

Having emerged from the Second World War on the winning side, the Soviet Union has since developed to world stature. It has been the most direct and potent competitor of the United States, its most persistent challenger for the world leadership role. It has a strong power base.

First, its economy. While essentially domestically oriented and therefore not a dominant factor in world trade, the economy has grown in size and is capable of producing large quantities of basic industrial goods and many consumer goods, even though of limited assortment and inadequate quality. In terms of quantities or global value of output, the Soviet economy ranks second in the world.

The military power of the Soviet Union is unquestionably impressive. It has the strongest conventional army, has developed a very powerful navy, and has an impressive atomic arsenal, with the capacity to deliver warheads to any desired objective. All of the above is supported by a good world-scale logistic system.

The political posture of the Soviet Union has also grown, at least in apparent strength. Internally it is a monolithic power structure without any major challenges. Externally, the Soviet Union has used to advantage a number of its trump cards. In what is likely to be recorded in history as the decolonization decades, the Soviet Union has posed as the champion of national liberation movements. It has offered a clear, sharp alternative to the societal blue-print left by colonial powers, or to that offered by the United States. To countries that have aspired to rapid industrialization, it offered a planned economy model, presumably capable of taking any country quickly through early, forced-draft industrialization stages. To ensure the "discipline" necessary for such an industrialization process, the Soviet Union advocated the unitary power system in the form of dictatorship of the proletariat. The above prescriptions were rooted in, and legitimized by, the official Marxist ideology, which continues to appeal to many around the world. The economic capacity to support big military power and the political ability to deploy it without much internal debate, enhanced the attractiveness of the Soviet model to those who believe that "might is right".

Despite such evident strengths, the Soviet Union may have passed the zenith of its power and influence. Its fragilities are likely to increase and its ability to shape the destiny of the world will decline.

At this stage of its economic and social development, fundamental restructuring of its societal order seems necessary, yet the probability of its being carried out in a painless, evolutionary way is very low. If, however, significant restructuring is not carried out within the next couple of decades, the ultimate consequence will be complete disintegration of the Soviet Union as a political entity. Support for these conclusions emerges from the analysis of the current state of the Soviet Union.

2. The Present Balance Sheet

Using the previously proposed way of analysing the effectiveness of a country, i.e.

$$\text{Eff} = f\left[\frac{\text{resources}}{\text{population}} + /\text{or} \left(\begin{array}{c}\text{will, know-how, societal}\\ \text{order, investment}\end{array}\right) + \text{ext. world}\right]$$

we can start by enumerating some of the key elements.

2.1. ASSETS

(a) Biggest territory of any country, spread over two continents, with access to different seas. Fertile lands, *very rich endowment* of virtually the whole range of natural resources, including a broad base of energy sources and even big deposits of gold. Though accessibility and climatic conditions render the exploitation of some resources costly, the overall *ratio of resources to population is most favourable*, making the option of autarky (economic self-sufficiency) if not economically attractive, at least theoretically possible.

(b) The *will* to work effectively exists in that part of the population upon whom the system bestows high rewards. This applies to much of the party elite, senior technocrats, and parts of the scientific and artistic establishment. The motivation of a large proportion of the population seems low, however, and needs to be "whipped up" by various campaigns.

(c) The range of *know-how* is extensive, particularly on the technical front, with real mastery of theoretical sciences (mathematics, physics, cybernetics) and an in-depth capacity in a number of applied engineering fields. The education network is extensive and diverse, particularly in natural sciences and technical fields. As a result, much of the population is technically well educated and its potential productivity is, therefore, high.

(d) Rates of *investment* have been substantial, and the resultant industrial base is vast. The quantities of coal, oil, gas, steel, and machine tools that are produced are huge by any standard, and the capacity to move these basic industrial commodities about is adequate.

(e) *The societal order* suffers from many dichotomies and mismatches; it acts now mostly as a "societal straitjacket" and is, therefore, discussed under liabilities.

(f) *The external position* remains quite strong, due to the Soviet Union's military muscle, a well-articulated ideology that remains partly exportable, the continuity of the people in power, and the apparent freedom to use that power both internally and externally.

2.2. LIABILITIES

All significant liabilities stem from the institutional framework, the societal order itself, and, particularly, the dichotomies between:

—the officially professed egalitarian-collectivist values and adminis-trative practices, which evoke individualistic, competitive be-haviour;
—a rather liberal constitution and the dictatorial nature of political governance;
—an economic system, suitable for early stages of economic develop-ment, and the economy itself, which is approaching the mass con-sumption stage; the values of the majority of the population are characteristic of this more advanced stage of development.

The above dichotomies have to be kept in mind when analysing the liabilities of the Soviet societal order.

(a) The *egalitarian-collectivist values* are professed and promul-gated as those that, while not yet fully operational, are desirable and the ones towards which the Soviet society is approaching. In reality, the individualistic-competitive values survive and are, in fact, re-inforced by high differentiation in rewards (both monetary and other) according to an individual's performance and loyalty to the regime. This contradiction seems to diminish the general will to work. The "patriotic" motive is diluted by differences in rewards, yet material rewards are inadequate in most occupations. Only the élite in the Party, administration, sciences, the artistic and sports worlds can remain strongly motivated, both by their capacity to influence things and by the high rewards that accrue to them.

(b) Linked to this is a poor conversion rate of theoretical knowl-edge and scientific discoveries into useful new products, processes, procedures. The attractiveness of increased academic respectability and scientific career prospects outweigh the lesser rewards and

greater risks of activities leading to "commercially" useful innovations. The problem is amplified by the fact that the majority of
people in the world's biggest scientific establishment work in central
research institutes, far from the industrial and market fronts. As is
well known from empirical studies, most useful innovations are "need
induced" rather than products of spillover of accumulated theoretical
knowledge. The Soviet Union thus imports some technology in a
number of fields, though not of course in the military field, where
clearly defined objectives evoke from scientists the necessary technical innovations.

(c) Considering the high investment rates and the advanced state of
scientific knowledge, the *actual productivity is low* in most sectors of
the economy.

(d) *Agriculture* is the weakest element in the Soviet economy. It
employs over 25 per cent of the working population; yet the country
has changed from the biggest wheat exporter a century ago to the
biggest wheat importer in some recent years—even though the population has not expanded rapidly and dietary habits have not transformed dramatically. The causes are multiple: scars from forcible
collectivization, excessive skimming of agricultural surpluses to
finance industrialization, hence inadequate material rewards to
peasants, insufficient modernization of agriculture (mechanization,
fertilization), intrinsic difficulty of applying central planning to agriculture, and, finally, the diversion of much of the peasants' energy and
attention to intensive cultivation of private plots, from which they
derive a very necessary supplement for sustenance and where the
rewards for work are direct and commensurate to the effort.

(e) The *economic system*, with its central planning and largely administrative allocation of resources, is by now out of phase with the
present stage of development of the Soviet economy. The "command
type economy" facilitated progress through early industrialization
phases (if one disregards the socio-political costs). During those early
stages the objective was clear—to create an industrial foundation.
The priorities were few: energy base, metallurgical, machine-building
and armaments industries, physical infrastructure. It was possible,
therefore, to make most of the economic decisions centrally and to
direct resources to selected sectors. It was a forced-draft, partly self-

feeding industrialization process (more steel mills to produce more steel, to produce more machines, to build more blast furnaces, etc.), which is compatible with "master" planning.

By now a broad industrial base and infrastructure exist and basic needs for manufactured goods are met. The economy is approaching the mass-consumption stage of its development in which sophisticated and diverse needs of a more demanding population could be satisfied. This, however, requires the ability to monitor varied consumer needs and demands and, thus, multiple points for making of decisions about what to produce for whom and how. Central planning becomes an impediment. The difficulty is aggravated by the need to impose the plans and control their execution, since most of the people tend to behave in a self-serving way, rather than voluntarily subordinating themselves to societal priorities—as should be the case if the egalitarian-collectivist values were in fact the dominant ones. The result is excessive bureaucratization. Organic pressures manifest themselves to decentralize economic decision-making, but this would imply loosening of political controls, which current leadership is not prepared to concede.

(f) There are also sharp *dichotomies in the political governance domain*. The constitution is fairly liberal and guarantees extensive freedoms, but power structure is monolithic and constraining. In theory, power resides in the population, which delegates it to its elected representatives. In reality, power is in the hands of party leadership and authority flows from top to bottom. The justification for this form of "totalitarian democracy" is drawn from Marxist doctrine rather than from the will of the people. These contradictions produce tensions, and it takes a big organization and much societal energy to contain them, increasing thereby the burden of "macromanagement".

(g) The greatest fragility in the political construction is yet another dichotomy. Theoretically, the USSR is what its name says: a union of republics. Nominally, they have extensive powers and even constitutionally guaranteed rights to secession. Destruction of the Russian empire and creation of autonomous, though federated, republics was one of the key mobilizing slogans of the October Revolution. Given the numerical strength of the Russians, however, and their traditionally dominant position, they have aggregated the bulk of political power and expect other nationalities to accept their leadership not only in political, but also in economic, cultural, and linguistic fields. Only those of other nationalities prepared to accept such leadership and work toward the creation of a "new Soviet man" patterned after the Russian model are co-opted into the power structure.

The above situation evokes strong nationalistic feelings, which are readily convertible into centrifugal forces as the Second World War demonstrated. Also since national aspirations to self-determination have been fulfilled in most parts of the world in recent decades through decolonization, such aspirations appear natural and legitimate to many inside the Soviet Union. These latent centrifugal forces are strong. A special aspect of this problem is the rapid demographic expansion of the Asiatic and, particularly, the Muslim population in the Soviet Union, just at the time of a worldwide revival of Islam as a vital force. This is likely to swell the ranks of "nationalist deviationists", which have been numerous in the Ukraine, Baltic, and Caucasian republics.

(h) An analogous fragility exists in the *relations with central European countries,* which came under the Soviet sphere of influence after the Second World War. Yugoslavia's refusal to follow the Soviet leadership in 1949, the Hungarian uprising in 1956, the attempt of Czechoslovakia to develop its own model of "socialism with a human face" in 1968, Romania's continued self-assertion, periodic restlessness in Poland, are all manifestations of national independence sentiments rather than of nostalgia for their prior socio-economic orders. This demonstrates the limits of the "digestive capacity" of the Soviet Union and, therefore, of its potential for further territorial expansion.

(i) *The conflict with China* is a very significant liability. It has three roots: nationalistic, territorial, and ideological. It is difficult for the Chinese, a nation of nearly one billion with a history of over four millennia, with notable cultural attainments, and a recent successful revolution, to accept the leadership of a younger, much less numerous Russian nation. Secondly, the temptation for the energetic, industrial Chinese masses to spill over into the rich yet sparsely populated Siberia seems great to the Soviets. However, unlike the Mongols, the Chinese have a meagre history of territorial expansionism. A nation bent on grabbing new pieces of land would probably not have built a wall several thousand kilometres long. The effort of moving such a wall whenever "a new piece of property" is acquired seems incommensurate with the "real estate" gains. Given the fact, though, that the Russians have been invaded in the past both from the east and the west and that they themselves have a consistent history of territorial expansion, the menace of a Chinese spillover into Siberia probably looks real enough to them.

An ideological conflict is also evident. Soviet leadership justifies present practices of material inducements and unequal rewards as a necessary part of "transient socialism", a stage of building up the material abundance base for the introduction of communism. The Chinese, thus far, have held out for greater distributive equality, even though under a much lower ceiling of material wealth. The above conflicts might be pasted over, but they are not likely to disappear.

On balance, the physical potential of the Soviet Union is huge, but its institutional structures are rather fragile and in need of substantial transformations.

3. Future Options

The directions in which the Soviet societal order could evolve in order to reduce the dichotomies, bring the various institutional components into better harmony, and thus be able to move into the next logical stages of economic development and political experience, are clear. The feasibility of such an evolution is much more questionable. The following sequence would seem logical for the transforming of the Soviet system: first, substantial economic reforms, then broadening of the power structure, and thus changes in political governance, and, finally, refocusing of the values.

3.1. ECONOMIC SYSTEM

Changes should take place in the direction proposed in the past even by some Soviet economists: from central planning through substantial decentralization of economic decision-making, to a "market-socialism" type of system.

Symbolically, the changes in the economic system can be represented as shown in Fig. 7.

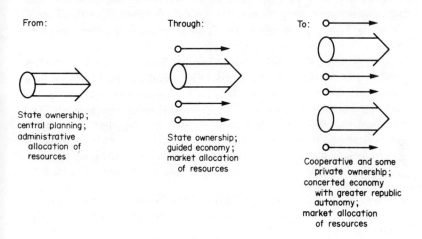

From:

State ownership;
central planning;
administrative
    allocation of
    resources

Through:

State ownership;
guided economy;
market allocation
    of resources

To:

Cooperative and some
    private ownership;
concerted economy
    with greater republic
    autonomy;
market allocation
    of resources

FIG. 7.

The evolution could go through the following stages:

(a) In the first phase of reforms, the amount of central planning should be substantially reduced and its nature changed. Its main functions would be to set key investment priorities, to allocate credits, and to harmonize forecasts of various production and distribution enterprises. Prices could first be brought more in line with real costs, scarcities, and demands, then gradually decontrolled, allowing the laws of supply and demand to fix them, first for consumer goods, then gradually for semi-industrial and industrial goods. What could remain under central control would be vital strategic items like petroleum, coal, gas, some key metals, and country-wide services like communication and transportation.

(b) In the subsequent phase the changes would be towards truly cooperative ownership of most industrial enterprises and collective farms and management of such cooperatives by elected committees. The system would incorporate some features of Yugoslav "workers' self-management" and kibbutzim. Private ownership would be allowed in small, particularly service, undertakings. Should strong popular pressures develop, property of land could, with time, revert to private hands through a gradual transformation of ownership co-operatives into joint purchasing, machine-renting, and marketing bodies.

(c) The economy, thus, could gradually evolve from a fully planned and controlled one to a concerted and guided one, using fiscal and monetary measures, differential credit rates, regulations about disposal of surpluses (profits), minimum and maximum wages, and an "indicative-forecasting" type of planning. In order to secure credits, avoid overcapacities and secure market niches, big enterprises would present their plans to the planning–coordinating bodies, which would compare them with those of other relevant enterprises, give feedback, and suggest changes.

(d) Most of the above could take place at the Republic rather than all-Union level. Resources would flow among the constituent republics more on the basis of trade than on the basis of compulsory delivery quotas at prices fixed by central authorities as is done now.

(e) Greater equality in living standards could be gradually achieved by reducing salary differentials and by using distributive instruments as, for instance, in Scandinavian countries.

3.2. POLITICAL GOVERNANCE

Changes in the nature of political governance are both the most important and the most difficult to bring about peacefully. The direction of change should be from the present unitary structure, with power aggregated in a few hands at the top, through broadening of the power base, to a shared power governance—without, however, passing through the phase of a countervailing power structure. Symbolically the transition can be represented as shown in Fig. 8.

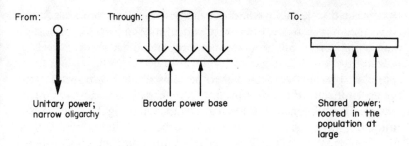

FIG. 8.

How could the above evolution conceivably take place?

(a) Economic decentralization, if carried out, would provide a trigger for a politcal evolution because it would bring about automatically some diffusion and decentralization of political power. This is why economic reforms would have to precede the changes in political governance.*

(b) The second major step would represent a gradual elimination of the present "dual" structure of governance in which party organs set policies and objectives and control their execution, and the administration (from ministries down) executes them.

(c) The above would reduce the power of the party and strengthen the decision-making powers of elected bodies and the administration. Policies could then be set and decisions made by those with popular support and/or technical competence rather than just the party loyals.

(d) In the next phase, substantial political liberalization could be undertaken by gradually stricter adherence to the existing constitution and laws.

(e) With freedom of expression assured, greater freedom of association could then be ushered in. This would lead to the creation of new political groupings.

(f) The monopoly of power of the Communist Party could then be definitely terminated by permitting candidates of various groupings

*Okun, A. M., Capitalism and democracy: some unifying principles, *Columbia Journal of World Business*, Winter 1978.

to be elected to legislative and executive bodies. The Supreme Soviet could then, for instance, elect the Council of Ministers, incorporating representatives of all groupings in proportion to votes drawn by them.

(g) The prerogatives would then be redistributed to transform the Soviet Union from a *de facto* unitary state to a true and voluntary federation of autonomous republics with equal rights. The constitutional right to secession would have to be resuscitated by resorting to referenda, and the likelihood of many republics opting out of the federation would have to be accepted.

3.3. VALUES

The main challenges in the transformation of values are: to eliminate the contradictions between what is officially professed and actually practised; to develop a set of values and a mode of behaviour that would reflect the new economic and political systems and facilitate their functioning. The thrust, therefore, would be from the official egalitarian-collectivist (and actually individual-competitive) values to group-cooperative values. Symbolically the change would be as shown in Fig. 9.

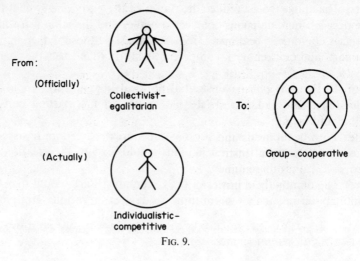

From:

(Officially)

Collectivist-
egalitarian

To:

Group-cooperative

(Actually)

Individualistic-
competitive

FIG. 9.

The feasibility of such a transformation would depend entirely on the success of the economic reforms and changes in the governance system and should, therefore, take place as a consequence of the above reforms rather than as a precursor to them. This is the reverse sequence to that suggested for the United States.

In the United States, spontaneous changes in values could occur with the political and economic institutions following suit because of the pluralistic nature of the country and the freedom of belief and expression that already exist. In addition, there is the growing recognition that the country is confronted by different physical and external environments, which require a modification of beliefs, behaviour, and institutions.

In the Soviet Union the dichotomy between the official and the actual, plus the inability to articulate new values publicly, imply that changes in values can only take place when economic and political institutions (within which people work, think, and feel) will demand and evoke new models of behaviour, thus new beliefs and values. One might postulate, therefore, the following sequence of evolutions:

(a) The transformation of industrial undertakings and state and collective farms into autonomously managed cooperatives would induce a proprietary feeling, a sense of responsibility toward such economic units. Members of these units would gradually perceive the impact of their decisions and work on others, and vice versa. This sense of belonging and interdependence would breed a more cooperative predisposition.

(b) With decentralization of political decision-making and reduction of imposition from above, the sense of commitment to things, groupings, and communities that people could then influence, would gradually induce more voluntary discipline and subordination to local communal needs and priorities.

(c) With political institutions at all levels opening the decision-making process to genuine debate and participation, identification of the people with their institutions could grow and preparedness for conflict avoidance and consensus seeking could be induced.

The above process would take decades. There would be some disruptions and economic inefficiencies. With time, these would be more than compensated for by the reduced cost of an oppressive bureaucracy and by enhanced feelings of freedom and dignity.

4. Feasibility of a Peaceful Evolution

There remains one fundamental question: Can the economic system and political governance evolve in the ways suggested without a new revolution, war, or other cataclysmic event?

Although the probability for peaceful evolution is very low, there are some factors that could facilitate the process:

(a) The need for economic reforms is evident. It is recognized by many economists; it has been debated fairly openly in the 1960s (Liebermanism); some reforms had been experimented with. Also, similar reforms have been quietly taking place in countries like Hungary.

(b) Internal pressures for reforms will increase because the growing complexity of planning will generate even further constraints. Furthermore, the already evident slower pace of economic growth will increase the difficulties of satisfying the needs of a more demanding population.

(c) Some external factors will press in the same direction. The fact that current growth champions like South Korea work with "concerted free enterprise" rather than command economy will be difficult to ignore. Continued reliance on imports of some technology will be an irritant. The need to compete on world markets not only with primary products, but also with quality manufactured goods, will also be an inducement to liberalization.

(d) On the political side it is clear that the Soviet Union is out of phase with recent trends. All empires have been dismantled. The example of Spain shows eloquently that dictatorial regimes can be transformed through evolution. Other countries (e.g. Brazil or even Chile) may undergo successfully this process in the near future.

(e) Internally, the "cost" of keeping the lid on a population that is better educated and more informed about external realities, and thus political options, will keep increasing. The contradictions between theory and reality cannot be camouflaged or explained away in perpetuity.

(f) Some of the Russians in the power élite are likely to start having quiet doubts about the benefits of keeping their power monopoly over the other nationalities within the Soviet Union. The key benefit they derive is the "national ego massage". But the economic and political costs of such dominance are high. Total management of a huge and complex system like the Soviet Union absorbs a disproportionate amount of energy, which could be used otherwise for production of useful economic and social goods and services. Keeping political discipline over the whole population means acceptance of many constraints on freedoms, even by those among the power élite.

(g) The experience of West Germany after the Second World War may have a model value. Germans felt that they needed more space to employ creatively their excessive societal energy. As a result of the lost war they were confined to an even smaller territory than they started with. They then concentrated all their energy on that limited space and as a result created an exceptionally prosperous economy and a politically free society. Some Russians seem to realize that exactly the same thing would happen to them if they would give up the burden of "managing" the Soviet Union. They might become willing to share the power more equitably with other nationalities.

(h) Finally, the fact that the power structure has evolved from an absolute personal dictatorship under Stalin to a power oligarchy, without serious political earthquakes, may be an encouragement to some of the élite to spread the power base even further.

But there are serious doubts:

(a) Russians do not have any tradition of a liberal type of governance. Leading others towards such a system would not be an easy task for them, almost like the blind leading the blind.

(b) Those now in the power élite would certainly fear the loss of acquired privileges and, even more, the possible loss of control over the liberalization process once it would get fully under way. The intervention in Czechoslovakia in 1968 was a good demonstration of such fears.

(c) Given the difficulty of an open debate, it is virtually impossible for anyone within the country to propose a master plan or a blueprint for the required transformations. Political power is too monolithic, too impermeable to any ideas that seriously challenge the status quo.

(d) The people in the power pyramid are quite old. Peaceful retirement may look more attractive to them than the uncertain adventure of liberalization. The recent (July 1979) return to tighter control of the economy is indicative of this.

THE MOST LIKELY SCENARIO

The probable consequences of the attempt to maintain the status quo would be more dissatisfaction, alienation, and dissidence; then, violent eruptions that would be amplified by some catalytic event, leading to the disintegration of the Soviet Union. As a result, most of the present constituent republics would become independent states. They would wish to maintain their independence for a number of decades. After tasting the joys and bitterness of such independence, they would likely voluntarily integrate into bigger entities, such as a United States of Europe or Central Asia, respectively, while maintaining their full cultural autonomy, as is the case in the present European Economic Community. A Russian republic would also find its place in some such supranational construction, the way West Germany did in the EEC—a strong partner, but just a partner.

Is it at all realistic to talk of possible revolutionary events in a country that appears so monolithic, with a huge army acting as a homogenizer for different nationalities and an internal security force that repeatedly has demonstrated its capacity to crush any opposition, even when large multitudes had to be liquidated or deported?

In chemistry, one can keep dissolving more and more solids in a mixture until the state of saturation is reached. A single additional crystal can then precipitate all solids out. Recent history shows that events can be precipitated in an analogous way in societies in which too many tensions accumulate. What is then required is just a catalyst. In Portugal it may have been a book published by a general. In Iran, which also had a strong army and a ruthless internal security organization, it was the voice of Khomeini, heard directly (as if from heaven) via tape cassettes. In Poland, the Pope, during his recent visit, could have triggered off almost any set of events that he would have chosen to.

In the case of the Soviet Union, the disintegration process could be precipitated by a series of developments and events of the following kind: reversion to tighter central planning creates more bottlenecks. The situation is worsened by a few successive bad harvests. The domestic production of oil peaks off while demand for it still increases. The Soviet Union has to secure some outside supplies. Doing this is not easy: it must bid up further world prices; at the same time it must buy large quantities of wheat; and yet it is not able to pay for either with exports of better quality manufactured goods. The temptation to lay its hands on at least part of the Middle East grows. The spectre of foreign intervention is evoked to divert the attention of people away from internal difficulties and prepare them for external adventure by rekindling memories of a Genghis Khan, Napoleon, and Hitler. But the move into the Middle East is countered and there is a simultaneous clash with China. There is loss of nerve, a resulting power struggle at the top, a coincidental major strike by workers, and manifestations by some "national deviationists". Conditions for a disintegration process are ripe.

The above scenario is not a forecast; it is a set of speculations formulated in a spirit similar to that underlying the earlier description of a possible sequence of evolutionary steps.

The Soviet Union is thus at a crossroads. The "map to the future" indicates two main roads—either a substantial transformation in an evolutionary way requiring great determination and skill on the part of the present leadership, or the preservation of the status quo with the likelihood of disintegration at the end of that particular path.

Either of the above ways will help bring the Soviet Union, or its successor states, into tune with the likely developments in the rest of the world and, thus, closer to the ultimate world order.

JAPAN

1. Its Past

Japan is a curious nation with a curious history. Its accomplishments have been among the most admirable and sometimes the most frightening. It is guided in its internal behaviour by an obsession to avoid conflicts, to build consensus, and to maintain harmony at all levels of society. This obsession envelops the many internal contradictions and prevents them from surfacing, from erupting too frequently or too violently. Among such contradictions: the extreme politeness, deference, and decorum of Japanese behaviour in all personalized settings is found alongside crudeness, bordering on brutishness, in impersonalized, mass settings; the loving permissiveness bestowed on young children is juxtaposed to the expectation of highly disciplined behaviour and voluntary subordination at later ages; while group, cooperative orientation is both the ultimate virtue and the normal standard of behaviour, intense individual competition at, say, high-school level is the norm and the price of entry into the right universities and, later on, into the right companies.

It is perhaps the existence of a number of contradictions and dichotomies, bracketed within tremendous self-discipline, that makes the Japanese seem high-strung, "under tension", and, therefore, extremely dynamic. I believe it was André Ziegfried who once said that the process of development requires the ability of people to place themselves in a state of tension to energize themselves. The Japanese certainly seem to be under tension, almost like coiled springs waiting to be released. This makes them very energetic, predisposed to action, to accomplishment.

The Japanese have known some sharply demarcated phases in their history. There were phases of massive cultural importation, followed by periods of isolation, digestion, and transformation of such imports. There was a nearly total isolation, lasting for over two-and-a-half centuries, which allowed the Japanese to reconcile and integrate whatever imports they had made with their pre-existing traditions, beliefs, culture, and to attain a very high degree of homogeneity in their society. Then there occurred a partly forced opening up, followed by a scouting around the world to identify sources of useful knowledge, which was borrowed or otherwise appropriated on a large scale.

In the late nineteenth century Japan carried out one of the most successful societal transformations in a rather peaceful, evolutionary fashion. The societal structure changed from a strictly feudalistic one to a modern, industrial one, which enabled the subsequent rapid industrialization and economic development. Yet, instead of destroying the pre-existing social hierarchy, the new government adapted it by assigning new functions to it. Some of the former landlords, samurais, became owners of industrial enterprises, which gradually blossomed out into business-industrial empires in the form of conglomerates (*zaibatsu*). The social hierarchy, loyalty, deference, obedience, and predisposition for voluntary subordination have been maintained, but tapped for national purposes, mobilized for modern productive industrial activity.

Having built up some industrial muscle and a military arsenal, the Japanese, feeling constrained and contained, turned bellicose and struck out to conquer the sources of raw materials or to secure future markets for their products. They repeated the cycle, taking on China, then the United States, and Southeast Asia, totally determined to fight to the last man. It was striking to see, though, how that same determination was redirected, almost overnight, toward reconciliation with the former mortal enemy. Having lost in war, Japan decided to win in peace—after the Second World War winning in peace meant outperforming other nations economically, as measured by growth in GNP. Within three decades, Japan was the proud winner of the all-time "growth championship".

The Japanese became extremely successful in the process of economic development by fulfilling all of the preconditions required for the process. The population was highly motivated; everyone worked diligently. Given the austere physical environment of Japan, work was for most a precondition for survival, hence raised to a great virtue. This traditional motivation was enhanced after the defeat in the war by the patriotic motive, the need of the Japanese to redeem themselves, to regain their national self-respect by outperforming other nations.

The second precondition, the possession of requisite technological and social know-how, was also fully met. The Japanese borrowed or bought technical know-how and demonstrated a tremendous capacity to absorb and adapt it to their own needs. They did have the wisdom, though, to maintain their own social knowledge, their own ways of running organizations, motivating people, and making decisions, to keep life-long employment and the seniority system, to use subcontractors to even out cyclical variations in economic activity, etc.

They have also fulfilled yet another prerequisite of economic development—high rates of investment. For three decades they averaged an investment rate of around 35 per cent of GNP. This was made possible by the traditional virtue of frugality rather than ostentation, hence high personal savings rates and credit financing of investments, since Japanese companies work with up to 80 per cent borrowed capital. Another contributing factor to rapid growth was the fact that investments were aimed mainly at directly productive parts of the economy, such as the manufacturing sector, while maintaining expenditures on social overheads and by the government at a modest level.

The underlying reason behind the ability of the Japanese to conform to all the preconditions for rapid economic growth is their particular societal order. As shown symbolically (Fig. 10), it is based on group-cooperative values, a consensual process in political decision-making (which transcends the formal countervailing power form of governance), and free enterprise—but a highly concerted type of economy.

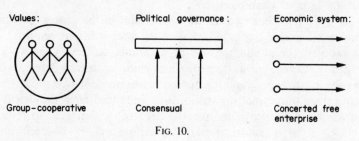

Values: Political governance :   Economic system:

Group-cooperative   Consensual   Concerted free
                                                          enterprise

FIG. 10.

As explained earlier, group-cooperative values emerged because an austere physical environment made them necessary and religious beliefs made them right. After the war, the Americans imposed on the Japanese a western-type, countervailing power form of governance. All the institutional and procedural trappings of it are there. The traditional predisposition to conflict avoidance and consensus seeking, however, heavily modifies the political process.

The above manifests itself best in the economic domain. While the Japanese economy is of a liberal, free enterprise type, it gives the impression of being a centrally planned one because of a high degree of harmonization of private initiatives, using as an ultimate criterion the good of Japan. The country has, therefore, been aptly baptized "Japan Incorporated". There may not be a full-scale "national economic symphony", but there is, at any rate, first-class chamber music produced by "the economic string quartet", consisting of the Ministry of International Trade and Industry, acting as the first violin, with trading houses, banks, and leading industrial enterprises providing the rest of the harmony. Priorities can be established, feasibility of conquering new export markets assessed, and economic missions divided up, without direct administrative imposition, thus without the burden of a huge bureaucracy. The system combines, therefore, the advantages of a liberal economy with its multiple centres of initiative, innovation, and efficient production, with some advantages of a planned economy, such as the ability to set overall national objectives and priorities.

2. The Present State

Japan has a number of outstanding assets:

—A highly motivated, diligent, disciplined, and skilled population with a mastery of technology on all fronts and the appropriate social organizational know-how for effective management of institutions at all levels.
—A highly diversified and productive industrial sector that evolved quickly from being labour-intensive into being capital- and material-intensive.
—A societal order and an institutional framework that enables the country to function well since its various components are in fair harmony with each other.

There are some liabilities:

—The country is virtually devoid of any natural resources, totally dependent on their importation, and, thus, highly vulnerable to political disruptions or even blackmail.
—It is also vulnerable as far as its export markets are concerned. Its

very success, achieved by concentration on a fairly narrow range of products and an in-depth penetration of selected markets, evokes not only admiration but also some hostility and protectionist moves.

3. Future Options

What are the future choices, the directions in which the Japanese societal order could evolve?

Its present set of values seems quite suitable for "the spaceship earth", which Japan had already partially experienced during its period of isolation, but which is a new condition for much of the rest of the world. Some adjustments in values could take place, however, in order to render individuals more autonomous and reduce the psychic cost of voluntary subordination, which currently may be too high. A somewhat greater degree of individual autonomy and self-determination need not be incompatible with cooperative predisposition. Small groups, work teams, corporation, or nation could remain the objects of loyalty and commitment. The Japanese could, perhaps, learn how to march to other tunes, coming from outside their borders, to interact with the rest of the world with greater empathy. The Japanese have tended to be too ethnocentric, performing admirably well, but essentially for themselves. Given their great accomplishment capacity, some of their energy should be redirected to serve the interests of humanity as such. Even if the immense reservoir of predisposition to loyalty, commitment, and cooperation were to spill over the national boundaries, it would not diminish the sense of national cohesion nor impair its effectiveness, but would prepare for the Japanese a more secure and welcome place in the world community.

When it comes to political governance, some constitutional changes could be made to provide the legal basis for true coalition governments, incorporating representatives from different political groupings. Given the consensus-building capacity of the Japanese, this should be feasible and would be more reflective of their values/ beliefs than the formal countervailing type of governance. A coalition government would also be able to connect better with the outside world, since it could then do so on a variety of terms.

Little change is needed in the Japanese economic system. What clearly has to take place is a quick restructuring of the present material- and capital-intensive mode of output to a more knowledge-intensive mode in order to reduce the dependability on inflows of large quantities of primary materials. Reduction of the import burden might also allow a somewhat different allocation of resources in order to improve housing, the infrastructure, the general social overhead, and foreign aid. Given the great surpluses in trade that Japan has been accumulating, it is obvious that the rate of direct foreign investment can be even further increased. This seems a better option than voluntary restraints of exports, or spending surpluses on inflated luxuries like art or wine.

The greatest imperative for Japan is to reposition itself in the world's geopolitical and economic constellation. Japan could turn toward Siberia to reduce the vulnerability of supplies of some of the primary materials. The underexploited resources there, in geographical proximity to Japan, with Japanese capital and technology, seem a potent combination. A rapprochement with the Soviet Union, however, would not be viewed with too much favour by the United States, whose military protection and whose willingness to absorb massive Japanese exports will remain of great importance for a while. The Chinese would not view such an entente between Japan and the Soviet Union with great favour either.

The second option is to turn towards China—an option that Japan is likely to pursue. The attractiveness of the combination is striking. China has a broad range of natural resources, a huge, diligent labour force, whose skills could be upgraded quickly, and large potential markets. The above, combined with the Japanese surplus of capital and the stock of whatever know-how would be required, could produce some startling economic achievements. True, there are memories of past animosities between the two nations, but there is still some cultural affinity, and the promise of the future pay-offs should more than outweigh past resentments. Economic cooperation between Japan and China, amplified in its effects by interaction with a number of Asian countries on the Pacific periphery that are already developing at a rapid pace, will create a significant new centre of gravity for the world economy. Though temporarily unsettling and even threatening to the Western world, it could provide, in the long run, another cornerstone for the construction of a more broadly based, hence more stable, world economic ediface.

CHINA

1. The Long March

During the past three decades the People's Republic of China has travelled a long way. The voyage has at times been very difficult, the road a sinuous one, the pace varied, and occasionally the country seemed to be marching backwards. Yet the country has grown along the way in strength and stature. It entered the international scene through the front door—not the service entrance.

The birth of the new societal order in China was a protracted and painful one. While four millennia of continuous existence can be a source of momentum and spiritual sustenance, it can also be excess baggage, a millstone around the societal neck.

In an earlier era, a rather stable societal order had evolved in China. Adequate innovations permitted intensive cultivation of the land and production of other physical necessities. Early development of thought and scholarship, and particularly the distillation and ordering of basic principles and virtues by Confucius (diligence, obedience, loyalty, respect), has provided a set of prescriptions for societal organization and behaviour.

While the basic units were the family and the village (a group of families), a sense of national cohesion was created by considering the emperor as a "father". The huge country was held together by a civil service (bureaucracy) to which people of all social classes could accede through open examinations testing knowledge of the classics. This system enabled the preservation of a culture and a societal order that were superior to those in much of the outside world. The philosophy exalting loyalty and obedience continued only as long as the emperor was sufficiently wise and benevolent. With some social mobility via the administrative route, power was based on merit rather than heredity; hence it evoked more willing submission to it.

Shared knowledge of philosophy, traditions, and principles of governance among the civil servants provided a common approach to
governance.

The whole system was, however, too firmly rooted in the past and
bent on the perpetuation of it. It discouraged any substantial innovation. When China was assaulted in the last couple of centuries by
Western ideas, practices, and, later, technologies and troops, it could
not respond by renovating itself (as Japan did in the late nineteenth
century). The societal order became dysfunctional and began to cor-
rode and disintegrate.

Sun Yexean, the founder of the modern nationalistic movement,
did provide a blueprint for the reconstruction of China based on
"nationalism, democracy, livelihood", but there was not enough cohesion left in the country to carry it out. Wars with Japan, skirmishes
with Western powers, and protracted civil war between communists
and nationalists brought the country to a chaotic stage, burdened
with massive poverty, epidemics, addiction, and corruption.

It is against such a background that the changes during the last few
decades have to be evaluated. The new regime tackled the core problems vigorously: satisfaction of survival needs, with more secure food
supply, some clothing, shelter, elimination of epidemics, basic medical
care, reduction of illiteracy, generalized education, some emanci-
pation of women.

After three decades the above basic objectives have been accomplished. No one seems to be starving. Beggars and prostitutes have
somehow disappeared. While for the majority the staple diet is the
proverbial bowl of rice with a few pieces of vegetable on top and only
rarely some meat, this is better than no rice at all. While men and
women are all dressed in similar drab "uniforms" of navy or grey,
that may be better than bare backs or rags. The very old wear the
pre-revolutionary black and the very young wear colours, perhaps as
a promise for a rosier future. Even "model" housing in prosperous
communes does not set new luxury standards, but everyone seems to
be able to live under some kind of roof, since there are no sidewalk
dwellers. The epidemics have disappeared and maladies get treated,
be it by acupuncture, herbal medicine, or a chemical drug, even
if administered by part-time barefoot doctors rather than by

medical experts. Children go to school and occasionally, at least in the city, to a playground or park. Everyone works hard. Everyone has to work, but also has the opportunity to work.

The above is a far cry from an affluent state or communist condition in which the principle "to each according to his needs" is fulfilled, yet it seems to procure a fair measure of contentment, and this for understandable reasons. China is huge and rather isolated from the rest of the world. It is, therefore, its own reference country. Most Chinese do not compare their condition to that of people in California or on the Riviera, but to their or their parents' condition a few decades back. For most, the present is a significant improvement over the past. They also compare themselves to those around them and their conditions are much alike. If there is some luxuriance it is well hidden, it creates no standard for comparison and aspiration. A curious phenomenon has thus occurred: a general feeling of relative well-being (if not affluence) has been created even though under a very low ceiling of material consumption ($400 GNP per capita).

The methods used to bring about the above transformation have not always been particularly tender. Heads rolled, skulls were cracked, the affluent "disappeared" or were brought down to the "common standard". The unduly independent thinkers have learned the virtues of prescribed thought. The substantial transformation in patterns of beliefs and behaviour was not, however, achieved by continued mass terror nor is it enforced by a huge bureaucracy. More has been accomplished by massive, preceptoral, saturation type of re-education—maintained by social group control within working teams, neighbourhoods, etc.* What may have been done with particular skill was to use some of the traditional virtues for new "revolutionary" purposes. Thus, while attacking Confucianism for its stress on obedience, loyalty, and respect of the established order (family, emperor), the leadership tapped the same virtues to shore up the new societal order to focus the loyalty on the work team, commune, party, and country. To get the work done and to maintain some cohesion, the regime can thus rely on some moral incentives rather than just on material rewards or on compulsion.

*Lindblom, C. E., *Politics and Markets: The World's Political Economic Systems*, Basic Books, New York, 1977.

There have been convulsions and jarring changes in direction. After some initial progress, there was the "great leap forward" with the folly of trying to build a blast furnace in every backyard. It took some time to put the economy back on a sensible track. After some normal functioning, with people accommodating to the new order and stability, the "great cultural revolution" was launched to purify the souls and as preventive social medicine, lest people start slipping back and yielding to the old bourgeois instincts. The cost of the cultural revolution was high: slowing down of the economy, destruction of some of the great heritage, closing down of universities. Almost a whole generation of learning was lost. Partly as a result of the above, the "four modernizations"—the new announced direction (agriculture, industry, science and technology, defence)—are patently necessary, though hardly possible to carry out at the rhythm envisaged.

Four millennia of history, a quarter of the world's population, and three decades of monumental changes, with a degree of standardization (uniform, unisex, unithought) never achieved on such a scale: yet, an alert visitor is struck by the absence of real oppression and by a certain perception of a basic kind of wholesomeness—not as a model to other societies, but as the feeling of a good proportion of Chinese for their current societal order. Is it because theory and practice vaguely resemble each other, with values, political governance, and economic system in a reasonable match?

2. Present Condition

As in all other societies, there are two sides to China's balance sheet.

2.1. ASSETS

(a) *Resource to population ratio* is fairly positive. The population is huge (pushing a billion) but so is the territory, even though over half of it is not of much use. The range of natural resource endowments is broad, with particularly large coal deposits and increasing estimates of oil reserves. Given the current rates of their use and likely claims on them for the next few decades, they provide an adequate basis for the projected economic development.

(b) *Will* of the population to work has been traditionally high and, if anything, has been enhanced. The diligence of the population is simply striking even to a casual visitor. It is rooted in traditional virtues, the survival necessity, and moral incentives.

(c) *Know-how*, particularly of a technological kind, is inadequate and, in fact, the country is by and large technologically backward. What can be listed as an asset under this rubric is the manifest intelligence, ability, and will to learn of most of the population. The potential for acquisition of the required know-how is, thus, very high.

(d) *The rates of investment* can be sustained at adequate levels mainly because of the political ability to "enforce savings", even though some 80 per cent of the population lives meagerly by agriculture.

(e) The *institutional framework* is relatively cohesive. The societal order is as shown in Fig. 11.

While the values may not be fully egalitarian-collectivist, there is a strong predisposition among the Chinese towards group, communal, societal orientation, and thus a high degree of self-discipline and voluntary subordination.

Although the party has a monopoly on power and authority flows from the top, the effectiveness of peer-group control at the base assures that the burden and cost of controlling everything from the top are not excessive. Political leadership has a high mobilizing power and the capacity to influence profoundly the behaviour of the people, as, for instance, in the field of population control.

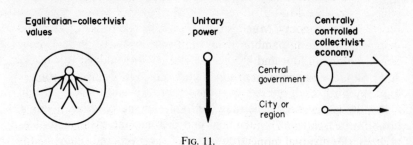

Egalitarian-collectivist values

Unitary power

Central government

City or region

Centrally controlled collectivist economy

FIG. 11.

The economic system, based on state-owned enterprises and central planning, with fairly genuinely collectivist communes and a fair amount of economic authority exercised at the regional or big city level, seems in reasonable harmony with both the values and political governance system. It is probably appropriate for the present early stage of economic development, during which top priority is given to the satisfaction of basic needs and the laying of foundations for the industrialization process, while ascertaining relative equality in the distribution of incomes.

(f) The position *vis-à-vis* the *external world* is strong. China offers a clear societal model, reasonably in line with Marxist ideals. It has followed, after the break-up with the Soviet Union, the self-sufficiency path of economic development, remaining virtually independent from the rest of the world. It is not vulnerable to disruption of supplies or closing of external markets. Furthermore, the Chinese traditionally measure time in longer units. They can outwait the others. This is a fundamental strength in our world, which is in such a hurry.

2.2. LIABILITIES

(a) *Know-how* is very uneven, varying from the ability to produce atomic weapons to the use of very archaic methods in much of agriculture and industry. These methods are suitable for highly labour-intensive approaches, but result in very low productivity and are an impediment to industrialization. Partial dismantling of educational institutions during the cultural revolution will have to be compensated for by stepping up the importation of know-how.

(b) Accumulated *industrial capital* and physical infrastructure are still very modest. Muscle power is still the primary source of motive power in the economy. Much is transported on the backs of men and women with flexing bamboo poles and on push-carts. People move about mainly on foot and by bicycle, and only secondarily on trucks and buses. Enormous investments will be required to bring the economy to a real take-off stage.

(c) The *institutional framework*, while internally fairly compatible, has some fragilities. The new values are not yet fully anchored or secured. If individual monetary incentives were to be sharply raised in order to increase rapidly productivity in some sectors, this could result in the resuscitation of more self-seeking behaviour with loyalties narrowing in on the immediate family, thereby diluting the collectivist cohesion. Political power is not as solid and monolithic as it might appear. Sharp changes in direction and constant references to the "smashing of the Gang of Four" are manifestations of political fragilities. It is easier for people to be loyal to things that are consistent and predictable.

(d) The current stepping up of pace and the opening up to the world in order to accomplish the overly ambitious programme of the four modernizations are likely to create bottlenecks, frustrations, and loss of faith. Developing dependence on foreign credits, know-how, turnkey plants, and joint ventures will limit the freedom to manoeuvre internally. Young students recite with conviction to any visitor that "we have to catch up to the rest of the world and therefore to learn from it". If sent abroad, though, will they be able to distil their learning so as to bring back only the neutral technical know-how and be totally unaffected by foreign values, behaviour, or institutional patterns? The fact that only a very small part of the population is likely to go abroad or come into direct contact with foreigners may reduce the danger of "contamination". The enormous mass of China should be able to re-absorb, if necessary "re-educate", or, failing that, discard those that have become overly exposed to foreign influence.

3. The Roads to Travel

There are several milestones that one can identify along the way of China's long march into the future:

—Internalization of the modernization process and economic development dynamics so that the process would become self-sustaining.
—Some adjustments in the societal order to bring its components into full harmony with each other and with the intrinsic characteristics of the Chinese people, which, while substantially altered through the revolution, have not been fully severed from their traditional roots.

—Stabilization of the society, or at least a reduction of the amplitude of changes in direction, so characteristic of the last few decades.

—Preparation for a genuine integration as a full constituent member of the eventual world order.

The first objective necessitates a number of measures, some of which are already being envisaged, such as:

—Intensification of technical education at all levels; greater reliance on professorial competence rather than "social creativity" rooted in ideological righteousness.

—Expanded importation of technical know-how to make up for the missing links in the technological chain and to close some of the more glaring gaps of technological backwardness.

—Gradual modernization of agriculture and, through this, release of more labour for the industrial sector.

—Expansion of the industrial sector even if some of it must be financed through foreign credits or by foreign investments.

—Expansion of foreign trade to get some benefit out of "comparative advantage" and to expose the economy to the stimulus of foreign competition.

—Increasing of rewards for innovation even if these rewards would go more to groups than to individuals and be of moral and not just of material nature.

Adjustments in the societal order are not easy to prescribe: an enormous amount of energy went into the creation of the present institutional framework and the momentum remains. However, some changes are necessary and their direction can be symbolically suggested as shown in Fig. 12.

Are the above changes feasible? When it comes to suggested changes in values, they may be possible because they could draw both on some of the present beliefs and on some of the traditional values. The traditional predisposition to loyalty and obedience, combined with the present notion of egality, provide a good basis for relationships of an essentially cooperative nature, at least within groups and communities with which individuals identify closely. The basic purpose of changes in values would be to render individuals somewhat more autonomous, less inseparably embedded in a collective entity. It

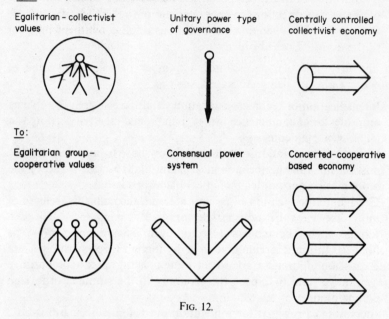

From the present order based on:

Egalitarian - collectivist values

Unitary power type of governance

Centrally controlled collectivist economy

To:

Egalitarian group - cooperative values

Consensual power system

Concerted-cooperative based economy

FIG. 12.

may be possible, after all, to "let the hundred flowers blossom" and "let a hundred schools of thought contend"* without them trying to stifle each other. Thus it could be possible to ease off the pressures for everyone to conform in thought and behaviour to the official standard of the day, without falling into the opposite extreme of self-assertion and self-seeking in a competitive, conflictual manner.

Such partial freeing-up of individuals need not create undue tensions and frictions, since during the last few decades the sense of national identity and cohesion has been significantly enhanced, even though linguistic and, in the peripheries, ethnic differences continue to exist.

Is it conceivable for the present unitary power type of political governance to evolve toward a consensual one? In the long run it probably must. The population is huge; the differences between

*Mao Zedong, speech in Peking, 27 February, 1957.

regions significant. Complete homogeneity and uniformity of approaches is hardly possible. Geniuses like Mao—with a great will and vision and, thus, the personal power to mobilize and lead such a huge nation—do not get produced, they occur. A second one may not be forthcoming for a long time. Even during his lifetime, there were obvious differences in views and power struggles in the party hierarchy. There is a need and, perhaps, a possibility to evolve a system in which larger numbers of people would participate in decision-making at the top, more in the spirit of accommodation than with a "win–lose" type of approach. This would create a greater sense of joint responsibility rather than having factions setting political traps for each other. The shared power system would allow various regions to move at different paces and with different priorities; in short, it would be able to cope better with the heterogeneity that is unavoidable in a continental-sized country. Another driving force behind such an evolution is the need for the political governance to reflect "the blossoming of the hundred flowers" that, by then, would be underway. Failing that, a serious mismatch would arise between the evolving values and political governance.

Some evolution of the economic system will also be inevitable. Once enough blast furnaces, steel mills, new railroad lines, refineries and fertilizer, truck and tractor plants are built, the next stage of development will have to be ushered in, with diversification in the range of both industrial and consumer products. In such a stage of development the economic objectives multiply and the complexity of planning and controlling from the centre grows exponentially. It requires, therefore, real decentralization in economic decision-making, more points at which initiatives can be taken, and resources allocated. Opening up to increased external trade—hence exposure to foreign standards and methods—will enhance the need and the opportunity to undertake initiatives on many different industrial fronts. In short, some decentralization of economic authority is the precondition for effective functioning of the economy in the coming, more advanced stages of China's future development.

Could the above mean a recourse to a free enterprise system? Clearly not in its classical form. Restitution of profit maximization as the primary objective of any economic unit and the individuals within it would go directly against the egalitarian-cooperative predispositions, which by then are likely to be more securely rooted in the people. Restitution of private ownership, particularly in industry, would be very difficult and politically unwise. Who should become the new owners? How to justify the creation of the propertied new class *vis-à-vis* the rest of the society? Would this not be a betrayal of the spirit of the revolution?

What seems feasible, though, is a gradual transformation from a state to a more cooperative type of property ownership. Wherever they settle, Chinese immigrants demonstrate a strong proprietary and acquisitive instinct as well as high achievement drive. They tend to do very well economically in all their adopted countries. Yet their proprietary and acquisitive instincts seem to be readily subordinated to family interests. Assuming that these traits are characteristic also of the Chinese within China, it should be feasible to tap these coexisting instincts and drives within the cooperative ownership structure. This could be more readily done if the economic units are small or homogenous enough to engender a sense of identification and commitment from their members, if the links between individual effort, group output, and rewards are close enough, and if the distribution of rewards is perceived as equitable. In agriculture this may imply a transformation of the present huge communes (30,000 people is not unusual); central administrative bodies would service communal needs such as education and health care, whereas the economic functions of production of food and selling of surpluses could pass to smaller units with joint title to land and a large degree of autonomy.

An even more necessary and easier reform will be the introduction of greater freedom of the market. This will respond better to the future need to direct resources to where they are most needed and can be used most effectively. In a huge country like China such functions would be difficult to accomplish through central planning and control. Some freedom of the market will also assure that economic units (enterprises, communes, cooperatives) stay above a certain minimum threshold of efficiency. The government would still maintain overall control of the economy by announcing key priorities, extending credits on differential terms, act as a big buyer, and set limits on some prices. It would rely more on voluntary discipline and peer-group control, sustained by continued intense effort in "social education", than on compulsion or cumbersome bureaucratic control.

What should occur in parallel with the evolution described above is some stabilization of the societal order. During the last few decades, China's leadership made rather abrupt changes in direction—"left, right, left, right"—with the whole society oscillating between the so-called "messianic and pragmatic" phases.* We know from physics that the greater the speed and mass, and the sharper the turn, the greater the centrifugal force. This law also applies to social phenomena. Another couple of abrupt changes and Chinese leaders could end up marching in one direction while the masses might keep moving in another.

It seems safe to speculate that the required stabilization would come as an automatic by-product of the shift toward a consensual power system. Consensus, by definition, eliminates sharp oscillation. The slowness of changes in a country like Switzerland is eloquent proof thereof.

The final—and perhaps most difficult—challenge to the Chinese within the next few decades is their integration into the rest of the world. Much stands in its way. First, the many centuries of aloof, superior attitude toward the outside. Then a century of humiliation by that world. This was followed by protracted conflict with the United States as the representative power of the contemporary world, plus the disillusionment in and falling out with the Soviet Union, China's ideological partner—turned into its greatest enemy. All that predisposed and partly forced China onto the path of self-reliance, independence, and virtual isolation. How, then, can the Chinese just step back into the ranks and start marching in tune with the rest of the world? It may seem improbable, but it is not impossible.

Normalization of relations with the United States was a big psychological barrier. The Chinese have jumped it, if not with joy, then at least with the satisfaction that they strengthened their position *vis-à-vis* the Soviet Union. The badly needed and officially proclaimed "four modernizations" not only make it indispensable for China to open up, but also legitimizes the move. The Chinese are confident that they can learn quickly from the outside world. But the

*Mende, T., lectures at CEI, Geneva.

fact that they put themselves into a learning posture, even though at first limited to technological know-how, creates a precedent conducive to future friendly interaction with other countries.

Smoking the "peace pipe" with Japan, and plans for greatly expanded trade with it, is perhaps the most significant single step towards reconciliation with the world. The trade-off was fairly clear: on one side, memories of wars and humiliation suffered at the hands of Japan, their "cultural satellite". On the other side is the cultural affinity and great attractiveness of the combination of the mass of diligent and intelligent Chinese (with a broad resource base) with Japanese capital and know-how. The power of the combination is obvious. For it to work, however, China will have to make some accommodations to a different political and economic system. This will be a good lesson in polyvalence (how to connect and work effectively with the unlike), the key prerequisite to becoming a partner in a world system—not a master of it, but not its victim either.

Should the Chinese follow, in their future evolution, some such paths as described above, the image that emerges is of a society:

—that is far from affluence but with some distance from poverty;
—in which traditional virtues of loyalty and obedience work most strongly at the bottom of the societal pyramid;
—in which individuals will have regained some right for autonomous existence rather than being just the molecules of a collective organism; yet
—in which there are still many constraints against aggressive self-assertiveness, both voluntary and imposed by social groups;
—with a government in which power is more broadly based, hence with less need for "smashing the Gang of Four" or other such leaders turned into "enemies of the nation";
—with fewer jarring turns in direction;
—with a somewhat more liberal economic system providing a better opportunity for the innate Chinese economic talent to be transformed into productive output; and, finally, a society
—that feels neither very superior to the rest of the world nor victimized by it and that is ready to accept and accommodate itself to the heterogeneous nature of the outside—in the knowledge that every

colossal, heavy step it takes will leave a deep footprint on the world order.

Day dreaming? Wishful thinking? Some of both, but only after screening out many other visions, such as:

—China going through further big convulsions? They may have had enough of these to last for several generations.
—China going to the extremes of totalitarianism? Once a society gets "ventilated" a bit, as is happening now, such an option becomes more difficult.
—China aggressing and conquering the world? An impossible enterprise.
—China changing its course wildly? It could break the country at the seams.
—China going into total isolation? The economic cost of it would be enormous.
—China falling asleep again? It just woke up. Its dynamism is that of a nation reborn.
—China thrown into a world melting pot? The chunk is too big to melt.

To speculate and hope that China will follow "sensible" paths in its march into the future is to count on a happy synergy between that country's traditional wisdom and current preparedness to learn from the rest of the world. For a reasonable world order to emerge some day, China must behave in some such way as described above. The least we can do is to hope for it.

WESTERN EUROPE

To many people, United Europe is an old dream; to some who witness its birth pains it is closer to a nightmare; to most it is more of a blueprint than a reality. Europe is a clear geographical entity and a continent with much common cultural heritage. Politically, it is two blocks, West and East, coexisting in an uneasy truce, and economically it is three different entities—EEC, EFTA, and CMEA (Council for Mutual Economic Assistance).

The fate of central and eastern European countries is tied to that of the Soviet Union. EFTA countries are held together by the common desire to maintain their political neutrality even at the cost of greater economic advantages that might accrue to them if they were to belong to the European Common Market. With time, they are likely to gravitate towards and integrate with the European Economic Community, which constitutes the core of Europe and its promise for the future. I will examine this "nucleus of Europe", plus Sweden and Switzerland, whose experiences seem particularly relevant for the future.

For several centuries Europe was a leading continent, a source of cultural, religious, and technological ferment. It has also been a continent with a high internal self-destructive capacity. The number and intensity of conflicts between its various countries is quite amazing. Given such a history, has Western Europe become by now a conglomerate of wiser, mature countries, or just ageing ones, or both? What is its current position and its likely future destiny? What role, if any, can it play in advancing the cause of a true world order?

1. The Present State

The economic potential of the EEC is impressive—provided the economic policies of member countries are sufficiently well harmonized and their comparative advantages maintained and fully utilized. The Community is not fully homogeneous. Its southern member and prospective members are at somewhat earlier stages of industrial development than the northern ones, having gone through their "economic take-offs" more recently. Among the northern ones there are the more dynamic countries such as Germany, but also the somewhat "exhausted" members like the United Kingdom. On the whole, however, they have a number of common denominators such as relative proximity to each other in economic maturity, the predominance of export-oriented industrial sectors in their economic structures, and heavy dependence on imports of raw materials.

Politically, Europe is not a picture of overwhelming strength. It does not have enough military clout; it continues to depend on the American military umbrella; and even the *force de frappe* is of greater importance to the French ego than to the world balance of power. The Community is not yet sufficiently politically united. Its voice does not carry enough power in world politics since it is not based on a common policy. Its responses to new situations and events are not well enough harmonized. As a result, Western Europe seems politically impotent compared to its past position and to its present combined GNP. Does the above mean that we can classify Europe in its proper place in history, give it full credit for its past accomplishments, and "file it away"? A tempting conclusion, but somewhat hasty. A very different picture emerges if we view Western Europe through the perspective of some individual countries and the probable future developments in the world.

FRANCE

France seems able to live with some contradictions and to perform reasonably effectively despite them. It has liquidated its empire without appearing drained. It is kept in a state of tension by ideological conflicts, party divisions, and adversarial relations between management and the highly politicized labour unions. It has egalitarian political mottos, yet also an élitist educational system used as an instrument for the selection and preparation of those destined for leadership—a real model of "meritocracy". Despite the rapid turnover of governments prior to De Gaulle, the loss of captive foreign sources of raw materials and markets, frequent industrial unrest, the eruptions of 1968, and the near electoral victory of a temporary friendly coalition between communists and socialists, the economy has performed quite well. Productivity increases have been consistently high. The GNP has grown at a rapid pace for prolonged periods. The standard of living of the bulk of the population has improved substantially. Its currency, after some shakiness, has stabilized. Its presence on the international scene has been felt. Its self-assertion *vis-à-vis* the USA and NATO, independent policy towards the USSR and early opening up to China, are but a sample of its diplomatic initiatives.

France's role in the construction of Europe is also characterized by contradictions. A Frenchman, Jean Monnet, provided much of the vision and a blueprint for the EEC, but De Gaulle and his followers held out for a Europe of independent nation-states. Yet we see Simone Veil as President of the European Parliament. The French held out for "punishing" their former friends, the British, for late entry into the EEC, while promoting close consultations at the heads-of-state level with their former enemies, the Germans. In spite of such contradictions (and partly by drawing some energy from the tensions caused by these contradictions), France has carved out an important position for itself within the EEC.

The recent picture is more sombre. After the oil shocks, a number of industrial sectors (steel, textiles, shipbuilding) showed their fragility; unemployment rose sharply as has inflation. The textbook liberal economic prescriptions, while sound *per se*, do not produce the expected results sufficiently quickly. They might work better in a country with greater voluntary adherence by all sectors of the population to national imperatives than one finds in France.

How then does France's balance sheet look and what are its future prospects? While there is a shortage of oil, the country does have some natural resources, a strong agricultural base, and a broad industrial foundation. It has demonstrated the capacity for significant technological breakthroughs (Caravelle, Citröen, Airbus, breeder reactors, Michelin tyres). Its societal order holds together despite the obvious stresses and strains. Values are very much of the individualistic type, yet strong feelings of national identity and pride evoke patriotic service-oriented modes of behaviour from many members of various élites.

The political governance is of a countervailing nature, with party politics a favourite occupation of many. The presidential regime, though, provides the possibility for rising above party politics and co-opting people into government on the basis of competence rather than just party loyalty. The seven-year presidential term provides for more continuity than in other democracies. The ideological splits are profound, and the present government seems balanced on a razor's edge, yet the differences within the "left" are too great for them to unite and tip over the present political ediface.

The economic system is essentially of a free enterprise nature, but indicative planning was a French invention and *concertation*, as a process of harmonizing objectives among free agents, is a French word, at least as used in its economic connotation. There are state-owned enterprises, but at least some of them (Renault) are submitted to the discipline of a free market and the invigorating bath of international competition.

Conceptually at least, the above system can combine some of the advantages of both the free enterprise and command types of economies. The important yeast and glue in the whole societal structure of France are its "meritocrats". They are admitted to élitist schools because of their intelligence, groomed in them for hard work and dedication, thus predestined and moulded for positions of responsibility. These modern "mandarins" with professional know-how are out of tune with France's egalitarian philosophy, yet they continue and will continue to act as an important part of the societal propellant—its flywheel and keel.

GERMANY

Germany has become the centrepiece of the European ediface because of its outstanding economic performance, its political stability, and predictability.

After the postwar reconstruction helped by Marshall Plan aid, Germany took off and has been flying at high economic altitudes ever since. This has been due to a number of factors. After the disastrous experience with Nazism, the physical destruction and division of the country into two, there was a clear consensus in Western Germany that reconstruction of the country and reconciliation with its neighbours were the overriding objectives. What followed were sound economic policies, modern machinery and a renewed infrastructure, steadily rising productivity, a resultant good export performance, growing solidity, and the strength of the currency. All of the above were greatly facilitated by industrial peace, in turn made possible by a traditional predisposition to self and organizational discipline and enhanced by social partnership between management and labour within the legal framework of codetermination. The country not only absorbed many immigrants from the East but later accelerated its economic pace by importing masses of willing "guest workers" from the Mediterranean countries.

"Social partnership", while still debated on the inside and questioned by many on the outside, needs further comment. Promoted by Britain and partly by the United States as a preventive medicine against the resurgence of a German "military-industrial complex", the inclusion of labour in management not only did not emasculate German industry, but rather allowed peaceful resolution of potential conflicts and enhanced the political stability of the country through the integration of labour into its power structure. How was this possible?

Although nineteenth-century Germany spawned Marx and twentieth-century Germany saw the Nazi totalitarian perversion, a quite different native tradition of values also was available. There was in some parts of German society a view of class cooperation that, for example, had led Bismarck to introduce the world's first workers' health insurance schemes in the 1870s—about 50 years before anywhere else. There was, in fact, an early ideological foundation for the idea of "partnership" between owners (contributing capital) and labour (contributing their work)—as opposed to a hierarchical and conflictual relationship between owners and hired, subordinate labour. The elements of the institutional arrangements that made the system a functional one include: a postwar consensus about the need for reconstruction; acceptance of the legitimacy and even efficacy of the free enterprise economy by organized labour; sharing of power through information and consultation with works councils; making decisions on key objectives and policies through the supervisory boards on which labour representatives could exercise their influence by participating in appointments of management boards without getting into operating management decisions.

The socialist government has favoured the distributive brand of socialism, helping free enterprise produce effectively and correcting some distributive injustices of the free market through government actions.

There are some clouds on the generally sunny horizon. The oil crisis precipitated much unemployment. Growing social overhead costs have reduced private capital formation. Generalization of code-termination laws has heated up some spirits and opened up some wounds. But the balance sheet and prospects look good: some growth in GNP, an excellent export performance, great monetary reserves, growing investments abroad, both in big markets like the United States and in coming countries like Brazil. The wave of terrorism subsided without precipitating the freedom-limiting reactions hoped for by extremists. The misdeeds of the last war have been partly paid for, partly forgiven, partly forgotten, and, by some of the younger generation, simply not known. The division of the country is painful, but the reaction to it is one of resignation rather than of battle cry.

The societal order seems reasonably in tune. Dominant values are of the individualistic kind, but tempered by some sense of discipline and an instinctive ability to work in organized settings. The political governance is formally of the countervailing type. There is some sharing of political power through the federal structure of the country, the ability of the more conservative elements to exercise their influence in industry, of the leftist intellectuals in academia, and of labour leaders on supervisory boards or in the parliament. The economic system is of the free enterprise type, but aided by government policies rather than stifled by excessive bureaucracy. The country seems, therefore, well poised for the future.

ITALY

Italy surprises by its elasticity. Other societies seem of more crystalline structure; under pressure some of their component elements get crushed. In Italy they get compressed or stretched and the country continues to function. There are striking dualisms in Italy: the agriculturally prosperous and industrially avant-garde north, and the underendowed and underdeveloped south; the biggest state-enterprise network in Western Europe, yet quite dynamic private sectors. There are a few firms of global stature and a multitude of small ones where the native flair for creative improvisation fills the cracks when they open up in bigger units. There is the most powerful Communist Party outside of China and the Soviet Union, yet three decades of reign by rather conservative Christian Democrats despite the spectacle of semicontinuous government crises. The improbable entente between the two parties to share in power, and therefore in responsibility, was almost consummated formally. If such an entente is to transpire in any country, it will be in Italy. As a nation-state Italy is young. Compared to its predecessors, the Roman Empire and the city-states, it has a short but spicy history. It embraced alternatively dictatorial and democratic regimes. It has exported its vigorous population to both Americas, it has gone through a highly effervescent Italian economic miracle that absorbed its growing labour force and, since then, it has again "lent" masses of able-bodied workers to its more affluent northern neighbours.

Not having the benefit of a world language like English, and without the predisposition to learn foreign languages like the Dutch or the Swiss, the Italians manage nonetheless to be among the first explorers of new foreign opportunities such as in the Soviet Union (Fiat) or the Arab countries (first ENI, then turnkey plants).

The dualisms mentioned above, the ideological splits, the industrial strife, and eruptions of violence show clearly that the country has not been homogenized. In a sense it has not settled down. Its societal order is a delicate ediface since it cannot be anchored in deeply shared values/beliefs. The predominantly individualistic values, the partisan political governance, and the mixed economic system (free enterprise, state capitalism) partly match, partly just coexist. The flexibility, adaptability, and certain ease of Italians when confronted with incompatibilities, keep the society moving. Much of the leadership, whatever their ideological convictions, seem genuinely European minded. This will be an asset to Europe, since the "elastic" nature of Italy will help ease some strains between less flexible constituent countries. The dowry that Italy brings to Europe is a colourful assortment of rich history, some present poverty, experience with various forms of political governance, a hybrid economic system, sophistication, and the art of accommodation.

THE UNITED KINGDOM

The United Kingdom is the mother country of parliaments, the originator of the industrial revolution, which transformed so profoundly the face of the earth, the builder of the biggest empire ever known. The transition from Great Britain—The Empire—to the present United Kingdom—a medium-sized island country—has not been without its sequels. Superbly effective in achieving its previous geopolitical objectives, it has been slipping on those measures of effectiveness by which others assess it and by which it now assesses itself. The societal order that served well in the past has not evolved much, while the environment of the country has gone through a real mutation.

Primacy of the individual has been the capstone in the hierarchy of values of the Anglo-Saxon world. The assertion and securing of individual rights has been the driving force behind the evolution of political and social institutions in the country, moving from despotic to constitutional monarchy to a fully parliamentary system with people as the ultimate source of authority exercised through voting rights.

Self-fulfilment drives found their expression not just in politics, but also in technical innovation and in building and running an empire that attracted the ablest for its management. Some of the affluent could exteriorize their talents in imaginative pursuit of gentlemen's leisures. A clear social totem pole and priorities in life emerged: foreign service, domestic civil service, with other occupations like industry, ranked clearly below them; the dignity of inherited wealth however acquired, yet some disdain for acquiring it through pedestrian pursuits like production or trade of goods. National solidarity and some subordination to national purposes were maintained by the challenge of external opportunities and accomplishments.

The captive or preferential sources and markets have disappeared, and spaces and opportunities shrunk. The mundane challenge of contributing to a better balance-of-payments position does not evoke the same quality of response. There is some crisis of aspirations since current feasible goals look pale in comparison to past achievements. Marching in unison to industrial tunes to meet the Japanese and other such challenges does not come easy to the British.

The nature of the political governance and the structure of the labour unions do not help. Development of a countervailing power system was a great improvement over prior unitary power exercised arbitrarily by a despotic monarch—a great step forward in the political evolution. In recent decades, symptoms of malfunctioning of this system have surfaced. The right to oppose is sanctified and opposition becomes almost a purpose in itself. It leads to polarization of energies, conflicts, frictions—a form of political-social entropy in which potential energy gets converted into waste social-political heat. This is reflected in changes in governments (not bad), reversals in policies like nationalizations or denationalizations, stop and go (bad), and industrial unrest (very bad), putting industry at a disadvantage in international economic competition. The emergence of unions was a necessary and right response to the abuses of the industrial revolution period. Their organization along craft lines, natural enough at the origin, is now an anachronism, increasing unions' capacity for mischief (a few can throw many thousands out of work) while reducing their ability for constructive use of power since, given their divisions, they cannot participate in the management of companies nor of the country. Labour is thus powerful, yet not really integrated into the direct power structure, its links with the Labour Party notwithstanding.

The economic system is basically of the free enterprise type, though with an overlay of state capitalism. Within it are several firms able to match the best in the world in technical and managerial quality, but the economy as a whole underperforms. Adding to the difficulties of proper mobilization of energies on the economic front, explored above, is the burden of the state sector. In most cases, firms or sectors have been nationalized because they were ailing. There is ample evidence that change in ownership alone does not improve the performance of firms. In order to be efficient, state-owned firms need to be subjected either to the discipline of competition or to rigorous and powerful planning. A real command economy seems an anathema to the British. Acceptance of the full rigour of a free market would be politically difficult. Voluntary subordination to national plans cannot be counted upon; in peace time its imposition is totally contrary to the spirit of the country.

The directions of desirable evolution are clear: more cooperative, societal orientation; voluntary subordination as happened during the last war; a national coalition type of government, as has been proposed by some; a better integration of labour into the power structure and, thereby, its mobilization for more productive purposes; maintenance of a free market discipline, but better voluntary harmonization of economic and industrial priorities. Is such an evolution likely? There are forces against it. Loss of position relative to other countries occurred slowly, almost unnoticed by much of the population. Great political freedoms and an agreeable life style will not be risked. Accustomed to being a leading nation and teaching the others, Britain finds it difficult now to spot and borrow new wisdom from formerly "lesser countries".

Yet there is growing knowledge of world realities, acceptance of membership in the EEC as one among equals, and a new generation to whom the standards of their grandfathers are no longer relevant and the traditional institutions less sacred. The unexpected new oil wealth could act as a booster to the determination of the British to realign their ranks and march faster on the economic front. It could also act as a tranquillizer, postponing the need for reform and greater societal discipline. Should the former be the consequence of the North Sea wealth, then the United Kingdom would emerge in a couple of decades as a healthy partner in the new European construction.

BELGIUM AND THE NETHERLANDS

Belgium and the Netherlands have many common characteristics and for our purposes can be treated together. Geographical proximity, size of territory and population, level of economic development, loss of colonies without undue trauma, high rates of increase in productivity and wage levels, are examples of such common traits.

The societal orders are also similar. While values focus on individual rights, they are balanced by strong concerns for social justice. Both may be more accentuated in the Netherlands. Both countries are constitutional monarchies with coalition governments—the divisions among "partners" being stronger along ethnic (Flemish–Walloon) lines in Belgium and along social–economic policy lines in the Netherlands. The economic systems are rooted in free enterprise, with Holland having flirted with indicative planning-forecasting and distributive justice. The main constructive lesson that can be drawn from the experience of the two countries for the construction of bigger political structures like Europe is that coalition types of government and, therefore, sharing of power are viable, even where sharp linguistic or political differences exist.

One could also extrapolate from their current experience to show how relatively small changes in institutional arrangements could improve the functioning of a coalition, shared-power type of political governance.

Let us take the case of the Netherlands. After general elections, the leader of the strongest party is normally asked by the Queen to become the prime minister and form a government. He then has to approach different parties, asking their representatives to join the cabinet. Before joining, candidates pose certain conditions for programmes or policies that the new government must either pursue or oppose, in line with their respective party's key objectives. Much "political horse-trading" ensues and, recently, it took six months to form a government. The government thus formed starts with some *a priori* conditions, constraints, and compromises. It is not easy then to pursue a policy in the general interest of the society. Instead of the above procedure , the prime minister and cabinet members could be elected by the parliament, with candidates in proportion to electoral strengths of their parties, but without any conditions attached to their election. The cabinet members could thus be at least partly "liberated" from the inhibitions of party politics and dedicate themselves more fully to the service of the country. The example of Switzerland shows that such a system can function very well provided, of course, that other institutional arrangements like direct democracy are also part of the system.

SWEDEN

Sweden, one of the non-EEC countries included in this discussion of Europe, has been chosen since it is the biggest Nordic country and the one eliciting most debate. Some see it as a standard-bearer for progressive countries, others as a prime example of "creeping, stifling socialism". It certainly has offered the clearest model of distributive socialism.

The country has turned around dramatically during the past century. It changed from a nation with an impoverished population afflicted by rampant alcoholism to a country with one of the highest standards of living, one of the most equitable distributions of income, and one of the most advanced social security systems. Nominally, it is politically neutral, yet at the same time it is among the most politically engaged in international affairs. It is very vocal in defense of "underdogs"; very much the citizen of the world and proving it by its generosity in foreign aid.

The transformation from relative backwardness to this avant-garde position has followed a strictly evolutionary process, with a slow but steady pace—a good example of a "boot-straps" operation. After healing its wounds from foreign adventures, after shedding the excess of its poor population to North America, the country started tapping more productively its resources like iron ore and wood, which were increasing in value. From extracting and processing, Sweden moved to manufacturing, and a healthy secondary sector developed. By the 1950s, Swedish industry could match in modernity and sophistication those of the biggest, most advanced countries.

What have been the main ingredients of the success? Clearly, these have included the development of institutional arrangements and relations that maintained political and industrial peace and that encouraged technological innovation, increases in productivity, the phasing out of noncompetitive activities and the development of those with new comparative advantages in international markets. The constant increases in productivity throughout the whole economy provided the means to finance the "cradle-to-grave" welfare schemes, raising the standards of the poor without crushing the rich. The above, fairly rosy, picture was reasonably accurate until the mid-1970s.

While there have been many contributing causes to Swedish progress, two factors can be singled out: the "Saltsjöbaden spirit" of labour-management peace and a distributive brand of socialism.

The meeting in Saltsjöbaden in 1938 between management and labour representatives provided the basis for subsequent, essentially cooperative rather than adversarial relations. The extra effort required for management to inform, consult, and negotiate with labour, and the fact that wages were pushed up at a steady pace, were counterbalanced by lasting industrial peace, cooperation of labour in technological innovation, restructuring of jobs and industries, constant upgrading of labour skills (the labour unions even ran productivity improvement courses), thus constantly improving productivity, and a real basis for higher wages and more generous welfare schemes.

The economic system that was adopted by the socialists contributed to the good functioning of the whole society. By adopting distributive socialism, they differentiated sharply between the creation of wealth, which at that stage they felt could be done most effectively by private enterprise (private ownership, profit maximization, and free markets), and the more equitable distribution of wealth, which was thought to be the primary role of a government concerned with social and economic justice.

Politically, the country was stable because there was steady progress for most members of the society, organized labour was integrated into the power system at the enterprise and national levels, and owners, entrepreneurs, and managers, while penalized by heavy taxes, were left with some scope for action, initiative, and decision-making. The whole societal order seemed sound.

The picture has sombred in the last few years. The social legislation/social security developed its own momentum, as did bureaucratization and wage increases. Wages were increasing faster than productivity. When the cheap energy bubble burst, the strains surfaced, competitiveness declined, and, by that time, the omnipresence of even a benevolent government began to weigh heavily on the population. After more than four decades, the government changed; a few years later a major strike occurred.

Despite some necessary pains of readjustment and despite the relative weakness of the current coalition government, the capacity of the society to maintain a relatively high level of effectiveness is probably still present. It resides in the basic ability to avoid sharp polarization and major conflicts, to share power, and to seek simultaneously both economic efficacy and greater equality without putting the two in sharp opposition.

The lessons that could be drawn from the Swedish experience, therefore, are that there are ways of sharing power with labour and that distributive socialism, if it maintains market sanctions, performs better both in terms of economic efficacy and social justice than "ownership socialism" (i.e. the model that postulates nationalization of means of production leads to better distribution of wealth and greater social justice, with economic efficacy maintained). There are not many convincing experiences of this kind of any model value.

SWITZERLAND

Switzerland is included in this analysis because the country functions well both economically and politically. Without any resources to speak of, it reached the highest GNP per capita among the OECD countries. Despite its smallness, four languages coexist within its boundaries. It is exceptionally stable politically, with very little social alienation. The key to its good performance is surely the unique nature of its political governance, which is therefore described in some detail.

Switzerland, as its Latin name (CH = Confederation Helvetica) describes, is a confederation of 23 cantons (3 of which are divided into half-cantons), consisting in turn of some 3000 communes. The cantons came into the confederation at various periods beginning in 1291, with the last created only in 1978. Each canton has its own constitution and a great deal of autonomy. The two-chamber federal parliament has representatives of four major and five minor parties varying from communist to rather conservative. The four major ones, with over 85 per cent of the representatives, form a permanent co-alition. The federal government consists of seven cabinet ministers, elected by parliament for four-year renewable periods. One of them is elected by parliament to act for a one-year period as the "president". He is actually just "the first among equals" with no special powers. The cabinet acts in a collegial fashion. In electing the cabinet, care is taken to ensure proportional representation not only of the parties but also of main language groups, regions, and religions. Since cabinet members are not appointed by a president or a prime minister, but elected by the whole parliament, they are neither the president's subordinates nor the mandated spokesmen of their parties. Their mandate is to serve the nation. There are no cabinet crises. The key principles and design features of the Swiss political governance are the following:

Heterogeneity—not melting pot. This is fundamental. The system of governance is so constructed as to preserve cultural, linguistic, regional, religious, and political differences. Despite the cultural centrifugal pulls from neighbouring countries (France, Germany, and Italy), there is great national cohesion, a "unity in diversity"; no excess love for each other, just a commitment to a set of political, economic, and social beliefs' to the forms of governance and common destiny.

Sharing of power. Given the existence of four language groups, two main religions, regions with different endowments, and thus different economic profiles and problems, it would not be possible to have two parties represent sufficiently well the various interests. Four major ones have emerged, cutting across language and regional boundaries. To retain the commitment of the various sectors of the population, they are all given the possibility to influence the system, to partake in decisions, and, as a counterpart, they behave responsibly towards it without forming oppositions that attempt to diminish the capacity of the ruling party to govern. Thus there is no polarization, no harsh competition for power, but rather sharing of it.

Majority accommodates the needs of minorities. This is contrary to the principle of majority rule in other democratic systems. It is not a matter of the constitution, but of convention, of common understanding. In order to maintain cohesion, the weaker must feel secure. Thus, even though roughly 70 per cent of the Swiss are German-speaking and only 20 per cent speak French, when people from the two groups meet the language will almost invariably be French. Power is considered to be more of an obligation than a privilege.

Collegiality—not individual authority. While cabinet members have assigned portfolios, major issues are debated and resolved in a collegial fashion through the building of consensus, in broad consultation with those outside of government who are likely to be affected.

Common men—not supermen. The president is only a *primus inter pares.* He has no more power than other cabinet members. There is no apex, no single person with ultimate authority. The fact that the majority of the Swiss do not know who their current president is does not mean that they are illiterate, but that the fact is unimportant. There is no need nor room for either charisma or superior abilities. The men at the top have percolated through the filters of service, integrity, and some competence. They evoke neither ecstasy nor hatred; they are just expected to do a reasonable job.

Diffusion—decentralization—not concentration of power. This is a natural extension of the principle of sharing of power. Even though Switzerland is a small country, it is not a unitary but a federal state, with much authority retained at cantonal, communal, and even district association level, not to speak of the various trade associations. Symbolic of this is the fact that Swiss citizenship is granted not by federal but by cantonal or communal authorities.

Direct rather than representative democracy. The right to participate directly in all key decisions is preserved through the medium of the initiative by which the constitution can be amended, the referendum by which a law enacted by parliament can be repealed by popular vote at cantonal or communal level varying from proposed increases in taxes to a new football stadium. If any of the governance bodies get out of tune with the concerned sectors of the population, they are brought back in line by almost twice-monthly votes on something or other. This acts as an inoculation against the abuse of power.

More interest—more influence. Some political philosophers worried about the wisdom of the principle "one person, one vote". They recommended weighting votes according to property (right) or education (presumed ability). The great variation of the participation in the frequent voting in Switzerland proves to be an automatic weighting according to interest in a given issue. The participation varies from 20 per cent to over 80 per cent. This worries some, but then why should people vote on issues about which they are indifferent? Is it wrong that only those who might suffer from the increased noise of the expanded airport, or those who might benefit from the increased traffic, bother to vote?

Power means responsibility, not privilege. When the president is elected, hardly a single person changes his position. There are not many favours to be handed out, no gains to be made. There is no great glory, nor even a promise of a big cheque for memoirs to be written about the scandals committed while in office. There is, therefore, no hypnotic appeal of power, little hunger for it, or little chance for perverse use of it. Only "absolute power corrupts absolutely" and anyone's power in Swiss politics is far from absolute.

Is Switzerland a useful model? The above "principles" highlight the positive features. They may sound idyllic. There are some darker shades: some abuses occur, wrong judgements are made, partisan views can creep in. The system is unexciting, lacking in glamour, unattractive to the young, and not very newsworthy. It is a "dampened system". It changes slowly, through marginal adjustments. This has some merits: it is not a swinging pendulum, there are no exaggerations, thus little backtracking; no euphoria, but few pressures build up; no exhilaration, but no gross alienation either through the loss of feelings of significance, as occurs elsewhere.

And, well, it works and has been working for quite a while. It is clearly one of the key causes of the country's prosperity. Switzerland's economic "miracle" obviously is not due to the country's natural resources, since there are none, nor to its numbered bank accounts, since the inflow of foreign capital is mostly a nuisance, given a very positive balance of payments, but is due, rather, to the fact that almost every Swiss knows how to do something reasonably competently and does it reasonably contentedly. Not too much energy is wasted on political friction, most of it is mobilized to produce something economically or socially useful.

Switzerland can, perhaps, be a model to countries that are reaching a certain political maturity and can start shifting away from the polarizing, friction-generating two-party system towards the shared power system. It has some lessons to offer to mature countries composed of different cultures, like Canada, on how to maintain national cohesion by giving constituent groups a sense of cultural security and a real stake in the system through direct participation in political decision-making.

Swiss experience may even be relevant for a very large country like the United States. The pluralism of which Americans are justifiably proud is not accommodated very well by the present institutions. There is evidence of centrifugal, polarizing, and even "balkanizing" forces in the country. As the interests of regional, ethnic, and other groups diverge, they manifest themselves as conflicts whose resolutions make some into winners, others into losers. The car-stickers in Texas—"Drive fast! Freeze a Yankee this winter"—have more than humour to them. The feeling of alienation, powerlessness, and lack of confidence in institutions is common, since they are too far out of reach for the common man. Resuscitation of genuine federalism, greater direct involvement in political decisions, sharing of power, and then responsibility, seem like good Swiss remedies. Since the Swiss borrowed some of the best elements from the American system for their constitutional rewrite a century ago, they could now pay back their political debt by re-exporting some of the elements. The Swiss model may also have a predictive value for how new supranational entities like a United Europe should evolve. Such entities cannot be built on the basis of hegemony of one nation, or a two-party system, or conventional coalitions (with prior conditions attached), with centralized power concentrated at the apex with a strong president. They can only emerge as federated structures, with highly diffused, shared power, committed to the preservation of heterogeneity, with the stronger accommodating the weaker and with everyone having some say in things of particular importance to him or her.

As the world becomes more synchronized and a single world order starts emerging, it is likely to have some such features. The system would not be labelled "Swiss Made", but it could well use some of that country's institutional component parts.

2. Europe—A Political Pilot Plant?

The attempt in Western Europe to unite countries that have been enemies for much of their history, to aggregate some political decision-making powers at a supranational level, without crushing, subjugating, or "digesting" any of the constituent members, is likely to have a predictive value for other continents. It can constitute a model of the transition stage that other regions of the world will have to go through prior to the emergence of a single world order. Europe, despite the slowness of its march towards political unity and the many obstacles in its way towards the United States of Europe, is a laboratory for experimenting with, and a pilot plant for testing the feasibility of, a new political construction, an intermediary stage between nations and the world. Other continents can observe and can draw lessons from Europe's attempt to create such an intermediary entity. It is a gratifying new role, a new mission for an old continent. True unity can bring to it many benefits. It is also a way for Europe to repay some moral debts to the rest of the world, to which it exported some fruits of its advanced civilization, but on which it also inflicted much harm.

Is the above image too much of a dream, a consolation for the current underperformance of Europe, or is it a growing reality? There are a number of concomitant, converging factors that single Europe out for the above role. First, while member countries of the Community are not at an identical stage of economic development, they are very close to each other. Moreover, their economic systems are all of the free enterprise variety, all with a significant social welfare orientation. The degree of public ownership and governmental interference in the economies varies, but the basic orientation in all countries is that of "private enterprise for public good". The economies are thus basically compatible with each other.

Even more important, perhaps, is the similarity of past political experience of member countries. The countries in question have had, and by now have digested, a rather similar political menu. Some of them have had more of a tribal and city-state existence, but all of them, with some different timing, went through building of nationhoods, conquest of empires, wars with each other, loss of empires, retreat to home bases, and full indulgence of national independence, with all the associated joys and pains. Given also the new reality of the "spaceship earth", the physical shrinking of the globe, the greater interdependence between nations, and the illusory nature of true and full national independence, many Europeans are ready to move into the next stage of political construction.

Another factor that enhances the prospect of political unification is that all member countries, or new candidates for membership in the Community, have similar types of political governance in the form of representative democracies. There are differences: some of the countries are constitutional monarchies, others are republics; some have a pure countervailing power structure, as in the United Kingdom, while others like Holland approach the shared power kind. In all countries there are truly free elections with several parties competing. Periodically, power changes from one party to another, but policies vary much less than do electoral promises.

There is another reality that, while adding to the pains of unification, makes Europe relevant as a potential model for the rest of the world, i.e. the linguistic and cultural heterogeneity of the nation-states. The only way in which a politically united Europe can emerge is by preserving its diversity, by integrating it, and building the new political power system on it. This precludes the hegemony of a single country over the future "United States of Europe"—of Germany despite its economic muscle, of the United Kingdom despite its past political experience of managing big and diverse entities, or of France despite the feeling of some of its politicians that they could manage Europe better than they manage France. A supranational power, to function at all, has to be drawn from its constituent members and shared by them, even though a Franco-German alliance could form the core. This implies a coalition type of government, representing the whole spectrum of political opinions, with collegial and consensual processes of political decision-making. A further precondition is the coexistence of a variety of languages rather than the adoption of a single "master language" into which others should fuse with time.

There is another factor worth noting: the drive to aggregate power at the supranational level is sustained by the realization that the current reality transcends national boundaries—that there are a number of key issues of human existence, such as energy, critical resources, monetary, trade and environmental problems, which can no longer be fully solved within the boundaries of nation-states. At the same time, there is a drive to greater self-assertion and self-determination at the individual, local, ethnic and regional levels. This stems mainly from a sharp increase in the level of education in all countries concerned, greater democratization of societies and, hence, growing aspirations of individuals to have more say about things of importance and relevance to them. Aggregation of some of the decision-making powers at a level higher than the nation-state has to be balanced by a great deal of diffusion, of decentralization of the decision-making powers down below the level of the nation-state to various rungs of societal organizations. The need for reallocating power in two directions simultaneously causes strain and confusion, but it is an objective necessity, not only in Europe but elsewhere also.

What emerges from the above is a picture of a new political construction, accommodating linguistic and cultural heterogeneities, based on more autonomous individuals, local and regional communities, governed by broad, permanent coalitions, sharing the responsibilities for decisions and also for their consequences, with economic systems varying according to conditions and current needs of the different regions of Europe.

Part of the foundation for this new construction is already laid. There are, after all, common external tariffs at least within the EEC. There is fairly free movement of capital, goods, and labour between member countries. Work is proceeding on harmonization of some laws. There is already a high degree of concertation between heads of constituent states. There is even the new, directly elected, supranational parliament, with limited powers perhaps, but of real symbolic value. Also, people tend to play the roles assigned to them. The more people get involved in European rather than national roles, the more they are likely to excel in them and relish them. The need for many people to cooperate, to accommodate to various national interests, combined with greater involvement in decisions at various levels, is likely to have some influence on the dominant values within Europe—greater predisposition towards cooperation, sharing of power, and responsibility.

In view of all the above, it seems legitimate, therefore, to see Western Europe as a continent from whose experiences some road maps to the future can be charted, and a design for the construction of a world order can be sketched.

INDIA

Because of its size, population, and past cultural accomplishments, India should be ranked among the leading nations of the world. Given, however, the current state of its economy, the enormous burden of its massive, rapidly expanding population, poverty, unemployment, underemployment, and the accumulated pains of past millennia, one might wonder how India does not collapse under this staggering weight.

1. Its Rich History and Current Condition

It seems that India's long history acts as a societal flywheel and a source of spiritual sustenance, carrying the society through even the most difficult periods. The historic continuity of India is as impressive as it is surprising. Its people are of very different races. It encompasses a number of distinctive cultures, languages, religions, castes, and customs. The Pathan of the northwest and Tamil of the south seem worlds apart, yet they coexist. What provides the bond, the cohesion, the feeling of belonging to something called India? Wherein lies the power of attraction and capacity to absorb and integrate into its culture so many of its past invaders and conquerors?

At least part of the answer must lie in the fact that, at a very early stage of its societal development, a spirit of great tolerance emerged for other cultures, beliefs, and behaviour. This was firmly rooted in dominant religions and philosophy. It made it possible to accommodate the great differences of neighbouring territories, which were at different times integrated into various kingdoms, without eradicting such indigenous differences. Everyone could thus identify with some part of the very heterogeneous entity called India, and this helped to avoid unduly harsh internal confrontations and provided a sense of unity. Could it be called "unity in diversity"? In essence yes, even if it does sound like an election slogan, which it often has been in different countries whose unity is threatened by ethnic diversity, such as Canada for instance. The experience of Switzerland testifies strongly, however, to the fact that when linguistic and cultural differences are not only encouraged but even nurtured, regional loyalties and national unity become mutually reinforcing sentiments.

Since the staying power of India is so strong, its prospects for survival must be good. The three decades since independence are reassuring on that score. Granted, the GNP per capita has hardly changed. Industry has not expanded as fast as it was hoped and cannot soak up very much extra labour. But the population has doubled in that period. This is the crucial fact. Who would have been

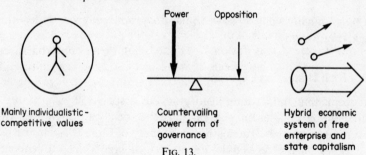

Mainly individualistic –
competitive values

Countervailing
power form of
governance

Hybrid economic
system of free
enterprise and
state capitalism

FIG. 13.

willing to predict in 1947 that India, already grossly overpopulated relative to its resources and productive capacity, would be able to take on an additional burden of 300 million people and somehow survive? The fact that it did, without massive famines, without major societal breakdowns, and even while preserving one of the politically freest societies in the world, is a great accomplishment.

But India needs to do even better in the future to be able to take on the second increment of 300 million people likely to be added during the next couple of decades and to improve, at least modestly, the condition of its people. To do this, India has to improve the functioning of its societal order. Its current complex order, even though it has many positive features, will have to evolve. Presently, it consists of the components shown in Fig. 13.

The predominantly individualistic values have some deep historical–philosophical roots and have been reaffirmed under long British rule. The ancient writings of Upanishads had already put the individual into the position of primacy: "There is nothing higher than the person."* This has encouraged individuals to focus on their own selves: the discovery of self and the search for inner perfection are attainable more through meditation and detachment than through action and interaction with others. In philosophical pursuits, the country reached early the loftiest heights. To some people, meditation became a substitute for action, which, combined with some religious beliefs, provided an easy way towards fatalism.

Not all Indians were given to thought in preference to action though, and many monumental structures stand as witnesses to the

*Nehru, J. *The Discovery of India*, Asia Publishing House, 1965, p. 90.

capacity to do, to create, sometimes invigorated by new invaders. Nor is Indian individualism of the pure variety—it could not be in such a diverse society. It is not only modified, but even counterbalanced by other beliefs that have been at the core of Indo-Aryan culture. They have been enshrined in "Dharma", a creed centred on the notion of obligation not only to self, but also to others. Each person was expected to fit into and stay in harmony with what was believed to be a universal order. Furthermore, the prescription "let no one do to others what he would not have done to himself" sounds like a paraphrased sermon of Christ, but is credited actually to Yajnavalkya, who preceded Christ by seven centuries.*

The notion of obligation, however, was focused more on small entities like the extended family than on the nation. Also, there were sharp contraditions between dominant religious beliefs or moral precepts and social practices. The emergence and tenacious survival of the caste system is the most despicable example of such contradictions. The very same society that reached philosophical summits pushed some of its members into the abyss of "untouchables".

Contemporary India, thus, has inherited a range of values, beliefs, and motives that is almost too broad to permit sufficient mobilization of energies. It is extremely difficult to build a set of political and economic institutions that would conform to all beliefs and expectations, and thus evoke the best in all people involved. Historical cultural richness turns out to be a partial handicap, diminishing current societal effectiveness.

Let us now examine the nature of the political governance and its difficulties. Indian leaders, before and after independence, remained deeply committed to a democratic form of governance in order to guarantee freedom, a notion firmly rooted in Indian philosphy. One finds in the Upanishads the following paragraph: "The question is 'What is this universe? From what does it arise? Into what does it go?' And the answer is: 'In freedom it rises, in freedom it rests, and into freedom it melts away'."†

Political institutions had to reflect the above. Given the political heritage of the colonial period, a form of governance was fashioned

*Ibid., p. 122.
†Ibid., p. 92.

after the British model: a representative (not direct) democracy based on universal adult suffrage, periodic elections with competing parties, separation of legislative, executive, and judiciary powers, guaranteeing individual rights and liberties. In short, a countervailing power structure.

The political rights and freedoms of individuals have indeed been greatly extended and secured. There is full freedom of expression (fully used). There is a high transparency in the political decision-making process. There have been no mass political murders, there are no concentration camps, no one gets sent to a lunatic asylum for defending the right to speak his own language. Except for a brief period of emergency law, there has not been much abuse or arbitrary use of political power.

All of the above is truly admirable, a state or condition to which many countries can only aspire. Is, however, the right to vote a sufficient consolation to the hundreds of thousands of sidewalk dwellers whose chief aspiration must be sheer physical survival, whose time horizon can often not stretch beyond the very next meal? How meaningful is the equality of political rights to millions of domestic servants who can cast their votes once every few years, but whose daily welfare, joys, and sorrows are so totally in the hands of their masters, some of whom find it below their dignity to speak to their servants?

And how about the several tens of millions of unemployed, some of whom with enough education to comprehend their extensive rights and their abject reality? Finally, what about the several hundred million mostly poor peasants for whom the next crop is likely to be of greater importance than the Westminster elegance of parliamentary procedures?

The luxury and partial irrelevance of the current political governance to perhaps 80 per cent of the population was highlighted by recent debates over the abuse of power by Mrs Gandhi during the emergency law period. For nearly two months, in late 1978 and early 1979, the energies of the federal government and parliament seemed to be fully absorbed on discussions of how to deal with Mrs Gandhi's case. Granted, she was a former prime minister who jeopardized the cherished political institutions, but she is just one out of 600 million people. During that same period over 2 million new people were born. There seemed very little spare energy left for the top leadership to worry about their health, schooling, and future jobs. While the small political élite luxuriated in what appeared as "excessive democracy", the destiny of the new millions was left in the hands of providence. This stems not from the democratic essence but rather from the countervailing nature of the political governance in which the ultimate virtue is to oppose, to criticize, to undermine—in short, to demolish politically the opponent, to stay in power or accede to power, to promise a better lot even though the chances of delivering it are slim. This is use of power without responsibility or, at best, with accountability postponed until after the next election.

The economic system, while somehow having supplied the essentials to the doubled population, is hardly a prototype of efficacy. Its weaknesses are linked to its hybrid nature: free enterprise with the public sector and state planning superimposed on it. In practice, neither the free market nor the planning are given a real opportunity, nor used to their full potential.* Free enterprise is partially suffocating under the wet blanket of excessive regulations and big bureaucracy. That even some family-controlled groups (like Tata) still do well is a great credit to their ingenuity. Public sector firms, while being ideologically preferable, can be born handicapped, as has often been the case in other countries, unless held firmly to rigorous performance criteria. There have been exceptions, such as Bharat Heavy Electricals, which not only grew at an exceptional pace for a few years but even passed some tough tests of technological and managerial competence in international markets. Many others, though, have been a drain on the country's resources.

The central planning temptation is fully understandable and even justifiable, given the need to recover from the long colonial period and to put India on the modernization track. There was not enough power put behind the plans, though—this for two main reasons. First, having chosen a "mixed economy" model, the country automatically put boundaries around central planning. Secondly, and more important, having chosen a parliamentary democracy, it was not possible to impose plans by force. It is not a coincidence that no command

*Lindblom, E. C., *Politics and Markets*, Basic Books, New York, 1977, p. 6.

economy exists anywhere in the world without a unitary power system (i.e. the capacity to resort to coercion); nor does it exist in any country with a countervailing or shared power type of governance, except during wars, when populations accept the need for rationing and control.

Given the complexity of India and its predominantly individualistic values, one cannot count on spontaneous concertation—harmonization of economic decisions between leaders of private and public enterprises and governmental officials. Thus there is a mismatch between India's economic system and political governance, and another mismatch between the economic system and the nature and diversity of values.

2. Future Paths

For the next few decades, India's primary objectives will necessarily be economic. In order to achieve them, though, there must be a significant increase in the capacity to mobilize the will of the people and in the level of their skills. The roads to those goals lead first through restructuring of the political governance, then some changes in values and in the economic system. The success of the last one depends on progress in upgrading the effectiveness of the first two components of the societal order.

Let us first restate what appear to be the key priorities for the next few decades:

—Stabilization of population. The addition of another 300–400 million people to India's population is almost inevitable. The sooner population growth starts tapering off though, the easier it will be to lift the bulk of it to a somewhat higher threshold of existence.

—Continued expansion of agricultural output. The country will remain too poor to be importing food. Good crops during the last few years have shown that India can even produce exportable surpluses. Physically, this could be maintained by the extension and improvement of irrigation, fertilization, by improved implements, and more rational use of land.

—Along with increasing productivity in the agricultural sector must go a gradual shift of more population to the secondary manufacturing sector and the tertiary service sector. The great challenge of the above is that the absorption of excess labour from agriculture must take place at the same time as some reduction of unemployment and underemployment. Whether this can be accomplished will depend greatly on the extension, improvement, and reorientation of the educational system, focusing on the acquisition of useful skills in all occupations to increase productivity and, thus, international competitiveness, real salaries, purchasing power, and effective demand. The motto could be: let every Indian learn how to do something useful, competently and efficiently.

—Eradication of the caste system and other class distinctions.

Given the country's present state and its rapidly growing population, the above tasks are monumental. How can a sufficient amount of energy be mobilized to accomplish them? How could, for instance, a "national service for development" be created which would mobilize millions of young unemployed and school graduates and put them to economically and socially useful tasks such as building roads and irrigation schemes or teaching illiterates?

Need India resort to dictatorship? This does not appear to be a useful or desirable option. Most of the Indian élite, which would have to initiate any changes in the nature of political institutions, seem allergic to a dictatorial system. Also, given the nature of the Indian people, a dictatorship is not likely to function effectively—it would simply get bogged down. A more constructive direction is towards the evolution of a "shared power" type of government, a true national government recruited from all political factions but elected and, thus, mandated by parliament rather than by the respective parties. The above evolution should be accompanied by a decentralization of political decision-making powers to the constituent states, many of which are in the category of medium-sized nation-states in terms of territory and population. Such decentralization is required in order to adapt policies and approaches to the diverse physical, economic, and cultural conditions of the constituent states. Is some such evolution feasible? It may be. First, there are great difficulties currently in India. There is some realization that the political system based on party politics is past the zenith of its effectiveness, not only in India but also in some of India's reference countries like the United Kingdom. There is also growing awareness of high economic efficacy in some Asian countries, like Japan, which opted for more consensual processes of political decision-making. The realization that there is a dire need for change, coupled with the perception that democratic freedoms can be fully preserved under a shared power system, may provide a sufficient trigger for change.

Some modifications in predominant values should be taking place, both as a useful precondition and as a consequence of changes in the political governance. These modifications should be in the direction of more cooperative predisposition, more voluntary subordination to communal and national needs. There is a great fund of ideas in the Indian philosophy, such as the Dharma referred to earlier, on which to draw for reshaping of values. What needs to be done is to highlight and resurrect traditional virtues such as the sense of obligation and the spirit of accommodation, as was practised in extended families, for instance. At the same time, the notion that "there is nothing higher than the individual" needs to have its pedestal lowered. Such a shift in values, like greater voluntary subordination, need not undermine the traditional tolerance of differences, which will remain utterly necessary to cope with the tremendous heterogeneity of the country.

No dramatic shift in the economic system seems feasible. What would be required, in the first phase, is to enhance the authority of planning, particularly at the state level, and have only overall coordination at the federal level. Better realization of plans could be achieved through greater unity of government, increased consistency in policies, and voluntary adherence rather than by further regulation and bureaucracy. Once necessary foundations are completed and a certain economic momentum is developed, a gradual shift could take place to a concerted type of free enterprise economic system. This assumes that political governance has evolved to a shared power type and values to a more cooperative kind, with greater self-discipline and voluntary subordination to communal and national needs.

One could envisage a less peaceful scenario for India: population grows unchecked. The burden of oil imports weighs heavily on the economy, slowing down development and increasing unemployment.

Monsoons fail two to three years in succession. Education, discipline, and morale weaken further. Tensions between regions and parties mount. The educated unemployed, having become more politicized and despondent, spill into the streets, cause massive unrest, military intervention, and civil war. India then yields to the totalitarian temptation. The above is not a particularly attractive prescription to offer nor is it sufficiently probable, since it is out of tune with what appears to be the essence of India's spirit.

3. India—Object of Sympathy or Source of Learning?

Given the overwhelming weight currently attached to GNP per capita as a measure of societal performance, much of the world has been treating India with somewhat condescending sympathy. The preceding few pages may have suggested a similar undertone. It may be useful, therefore, to take a brief look at the other face of India: India as a land of profound thoughts, as the land of dominant religion–philosophy, Hinduism, defined by Mahatma Gandhi as "search for truth through nonviolent means", India as the birthplace of Buddhism, which points to the "middle path", the "golden mean", a philosophy that could facilitate the accommodation of presently conflicting societal orders and, in the distant future, their convergence to some golden mean. Even contemporary India, despite its low economic status, despite the weaknesses of its political system, as a political entity is of a certain model value as a precursor of things to come elsewhere. India is, after all, a continental-sized country with a continental-sized population of enormous cultural, ethnic, and other diversities; yet all accommodated under the same political roof, without hegemony by a single ethnic group, without having passed its people through a melting-pot or homogenizer or political extrusion press to produce Indians of standard shape. Is this not, after all, what Western European countries are aspiring to, and what the ultimate destiny of the whole world is?

BRAZIL

Brazil is clearly a candidate for a breakthrough to a position of real significance in the world economy and of real influence in world politics within the next few decades. It has a number of factors in its favour but also some handicaps.

1. Its Recent Start

Brazil's economy has become fairly diversified and integrated only recently. For over four centuries after its discovery, Brazil, because of its natural richness, went through a series of distinctive economic cycles, each dominated by a single export product from a different region of the country. The products were wood, sugarcane, gold, rubber, and coffee, with other "lesser" products like cotton and cacao coming into prominence for brief periods and playing secondary roles. During each cycle, Brazil was nearly a monoeconomy, oriented toward the outside world and serving the world's demands.

In the last few decades, a significant shift has occurred towards mining and manufacturing activities, and full economic development was thus initiated. Relocating the capital from Rio to the specially constructed Brasilia, intended to orient the country inwards, was more a symbolic coincidence than a cause of the start of a new economic development phase. This early part of the take-off stage has been managed with quite some skill and at times even with a certain virtuosity of economic macromanagement, enough to make Brazil a good case study. The economic formula that Brazil adopted is similar to what some Western European countries did a century ago: encouragement of investments in mining, metal-working and manufacturing, and building up of some necessary physical and administrative infrastructures. The process is expected to attract more and more people from less-productive agriculture to more-productive industrial sectors, which can offer higher wages, increasing thereby the purchasing power of the working population and, thus, internal demands for goods. This, in turn, should provide the stimulus for further investments. Once a certain threshold is passed the process should be self-sustaining. It should work like an expanding wave in a pond, gradually spreading over most of the pond's surface, i.e. with time transferring the bulk of the working population from agriculture to secondary manufacturing and, later, partly to the tertiary, service sectors. The small percentage of the population that would remain in agriculture should also become more productive and wealthier through modernization (mechanization, fertilization, irrigation, storage), made possible by necessary supplies from the expanded industrial sector.

This process seems off to a good start. However, there are two elements in Brazil with which the Western European countries were not confronted when they were starting the modernization process: rapid population growth and the "transistor revolution", enabling instant and widespread communication.

In most European countries the population grew relatively slowly, taking about a century to double. As industry expanded and new jobs were created, labour was siphoned off from agriculture. Also, while significant inequalities in the standards of living existed between different sectors of the population, these were not unduly explosive. The mass of the population was not overly educated or overly informed, their aspirations did not grow too rapidly, while, on the other hand, some progress was visible. The educated élite could thus manage the masses.

In Brazil the population doubles in some two-and-a-half decades. Even relatively rapid expansion of industrial enclaves like Sao Paulo does not keep up with the pace of demographic expansion. There is, therefore, significant economic dualism in Brazil, with the privileged, wealthy modern sector comprising less than a third of the population and the backward and poor constituting the remaining two-thirds. Those not touched by the industrialization process are now, however, "plugged" into the rest of the country and part of the outside world via the transistor. They have some notions of standards elsewhere; they can aspire to better things and many do. This makes for an explosive mixture. The difficulty of Brazil's prior countervailing power type of governance, patterned after the American model, to manage the situation becomes fairly understandable. It is easy for any demagogue to bid up promises (which cannot be fulfilled) in order to get elected. The tensions resulting from the frustration of unfulfilled aspirations are not easy to release through normal democratic processes. "The totalitarian temptation", in the form of a military government in order to contain the pressures, is thus also understandable, although not something that most Westerners welcome with applause.

2. Its Present State

Brazil of today is a country with individualistic competitive values, a unitary power type of political governance, and a free enterprise economic system, with the heavy hand of the government guiding it.

2.1. ASSETS

—A territory approaching that of the United States, much of it still untapped but most of it usable.
—Huge amounts of some natural resources.
—A sizeable and rapidly expanding industrial enclave.
—A momentum of modernization and industrialization that appears sustainable, particularly because of the successful fusion and peaceful coexistence of the different constituent races, and faith of the country's industrial and professional élite in the country's destiny.

2.2. LIABILITIES

—Inadequate deposits of petroleum. Providence has not been overly generous to Brazil with this currently most critical resource. Given the climatic conditions, however, biomass holds out a greater promise in Brazil than in most other countries as a potential substitute for petroleum.
—A huge foreign debt, incurred mainly because of massive imports of petroleum.
—The population growth, which is too great to be smoothly absorbed into the modern sector.
—The dual nature of the economy, which is likely to lead to social and political conflicts.

3. Future Options

The demographic menace will hang over Brazil for the next three decades or so. It will be almost impossible to taper off the population growth before it doubles again from the present 110 million. Given this fact and the nature of the present societal order, what might be some of the roads that could lead Brazil into the promising twenty-first century?

Values are not likely to be fundamentally transformed. Because of its great spaces, the abundance of natural wealth and mostly pleasant climate, the predisposition to self-fulfilment, if not self-indulgence, is likely to persist for a while. A shift toward Calvinist attitudes ("you can do anything, provided you do not enjoy it"), voluntary subordination to higher purposes, and, thus, cooperative or collectivist values, is not for tomorrow.

A dramatic change of the economic system does not appear easy either. A true command-state enterprise economy with public ownership of means of production is not likely to succeed in Brazil. It is not compatible with the effervescent, exteriorizing, enterprising character of so many Brazilians. It would eliminate direct foreign investments, which have been of real importance for priming Brazil's economic pump. It would dislocate foreign trade and necessitate its sharp reorientation toward new markets. Finally, to impose such changes and maintain the necessary discipline would require an even tougher political regime than the present one. It would be like putting a heavy wet blanket over sunny Brazil.

What about the nature of its political governance? The pressures are on and the promises are out to revert soon to a countervailing type of democracy with parties competing for power. This may not happen, but even if it does it is not likely to last. Given the dualism of the Brazilian economy and society, and the underlying pressures, amplified by promises of modernization, the countervailing type of governance would sharply polarize the population, lead to greater frictions, and an explosion in the form of revolution or another military coup. Is continuation of a military regime the only way of containing the pressures until the rate of industrialization surpasses that of the population growth? There may be another option—a gradual coopting into the present power structure of people of different political orientations and creation of a coalition type of governance without going through the countervailing power phase of political evolution.

To prevent the coalition government from becoming a self-perpetuating power oligarchy, the government should be elected by parliament and be responsible to it. To further guarantee democratic freedoms (i.e. of expression, association, legal protection) and to assure that the government stays in tune with the population, frequent referenda should be used. Some decentralization of political power could take place to revert to the federal nature of the country as it was originally intended and as the vastness and diversity of the country demands.

Of crucial importance to Brazil is the necessity for relations between government, business, and emancipated labour leaders to take on a consultative and cooperative rather than adversarial nature. In this respect, the experiences of countries like Germany or Japan are more relevant for Brazil than that of the United States, which has been one of the reference countries. Since some of Brazil's exports are being reoriented toward the "new growth champions", so should be some of its political and social antennae.

CHAPTER 3

The Origin of Man and His Ideologies

WHY did different societal orders emerge? What were the sources of values? What inspired their emergence? Societal orders have been moulded to satisfy the perceived needs of men. These stem from the intrinsic, yet varied nature of man, which was at least partly built into him in the act of his creation. The perpetual philosophical challenge is to pierce through the mystery of man's true origin, to understand fully his nature and his needs in order to create relations, and build institutions that will enable man to attain his destiny, his mission, or to fulfil himself. The urge to understand the true meaning of his own existence in relation to the physical world surrounding him has been the drive behind the creation of myths, the structuring of religions, and the discovery of the scientific method. The search for "truth" diverged; the answers vary. What have been the main currents of thought? They can be presented in a highly schematized form (Table 3).

Let us explore these different beliefs. Most of the ancient myths and organized religions attribute man's origin to some supernatural power; they see him as a product of the Divine Will. In the process of creation, man has been endowed with a variety of attributes or traits. His behaviour is not, however, fully preprogrammed, hence it differs from that of his fellowmen. Its manifestations are seen by others as "good", "bad", or "both".

Ancient philosophers attributed man's behaviour to his intrinsic nature. Hsun-tzu held that "man's nature is evil; goodness is the result of conscious activity".* By conscious activity he meant essentially instruction, learning. The intrinsically evil nature of man had to

---

*Hsun-tzu, *The Works of Hsun-tzu*, translated from the Chinese by Homer H. Dubs, AMS Press, New York, 1976.

TABLE 3

Origin of man	His nature	Source of values "ethics"	Resulting values
Divine Will	Evil; Good; or both	Divine Revelation	Individualistic-competitive, or Group-cooperative
Product of natural evolution	Good; product of environment	Laws of nature	Group-cooperative, or Egalitarian-collectivist
Biological accident	Composite; his unique-ness = knowledge	Himself; the objective need	Not "pre-wired"; free to choose

be straightened out, transformed through education and inculcation of ritual principles. This he saw as the purpose of a societal order of "civilization". The sages were required in order to create the ritual principles and the sage kings to uphold them.

In a much more recent period, and starting with a very different base of observation, Sigmund Freud arrived at somewhat similar conclusions about the nature of man.* He felt that man's instinctive drive for sensual satisfaction is in conflict with the basic purposes of civilization, i.e. controlling the forces of nature for man's good and regulating relations between people, especially those relations pertaining to the distribution of wealth. Instinctive drives induce people to use each other as objects for the satisfaction of their own needs. This is contrary to the spirit of necessary civilizational regulations; therefore, these have to be imposed by a minority that somehow acquires the means of coercion, though ideally such a minority would master its own instinctive drives.

The questions that remain unanswered in both of the above philosophies are: If man's nature is intrinsically evil, where does the drive to improve, to create ritual principles, to master instincts—the drive for civilization—come from? From outside of man? Why and how do the sages emerge?

*Freud, S., *The Future of an Illusion* (edited by J. Strachey), W. W. Norton, New York, 1975.

Mencius held the opposite view: he felt that man was intrinsically good: "The tendency of human nature to do good is like that of water to flow downwards".* He felt that man possesses the basic virtues and that they need only be nurtured in order to manifest themselves to others as desirable behaviour. These virtues are: compassion, manifested as humanity; shame, leading to righteousness; a sense of courtesy converted into decorum; and the sense of right and wrong as the beginning of wisdom. To Mencius, man is only induced to do evil by circumstances, like a bad ruler. Somewhat similar views were articulated later by Jean-Jacques Rousseau.

The question that arises is: Since circumstances are the products of man, how or why do the "evil circumstances" arise?

A contemporary and pupil of Mencius, Kao-Tzu, saw man's nature as neutral, not predisposed to good or bad—it can be turned to good or bad.† This position is the most tenable one since we have ample manifestations throughout history of the same individuals and communities being capable of both very good and very bad deeds. It may be even more correct, though, to see man as endowed with predispositions toward good and bad rather than as neutral. The good and bad in him is evoked by complex circumstances, the interplay of his instincts and his interaction with other people. The main religions embraced a similar view of the nature of man; one of their purposes has been to evoke the good in man by codes, prescriptions, promises of reward, or threats of punishment.

If the true nature of man remains a mystery, the very purpose of man's existence is even more of a mystery. In order to understand this purpose, to know what to strive for, how to do it, how to relate with others or with the surrounding nature, to know what is good or bad, what is right or wrong, man has been trying to pierce the mystery of creation, to fathom the will of the Creator, to derive from it a just order and a code of behaviour. The source of ethics has been thought to be outside of man, a matter not of free choice by man, but rather of correct interpretation of divine intentions facilitated by revelations through various prophets.

The second, more recent school of thought about man's origins, is

* *Works of Mencius* (edited by J. Legge), Dover Publications, New York, 1970.
† *Ibid.*

the materialistic one. It holds that man is a product of physical evolution guided by the laws of nature, like all other creations. His nature, his behaviour, his history, and his destiny are all subject to these laws of evolution. Man must seek to "discover" these natural laws, to develop a rational understanding of them, and then to evolve codes of prescriptions in conformance with them. It follows again, therefore, that man does not have the freedom of choice of values; they have been predetermined for him. The certitude that some have about the ultimate outcome of societal evolution (i.e. a universal classless society) is easy to understand in the context of this system of thought.

The most recent school of thought, as articulated by Jacques Monod, holds that man is simply a product of accidental biological mutation.* With perhaps a somewhat unscientific finality, he asserts that modern science and particularly molecular biology has irrevocably destroyed the notion that man is a product of some Divine Intervention or of natural evolution. According to Monod there is no ultimate purpose, no fixed alliance between man and the rest of creation. These conclusions are based on the following observations:

—"The one universal and essential characteristic of living things is the conservativeness of the chemical structure (DNA), wherein the genetic code is written."
—"Evolution is not an inherent tendency of living beings."
—"Changes in the biosphere come through random perturbations which affect single molecules and are therefore unpredictable and uncontrollable in their effects."

His further observation is that social animals other than man are genetically predetermined in their behaviour through "pre-wiring" of their nervous systems. Their relations, their interactions, and the stability of their "social" institutions are thus genetically assured and perpetuated. They need no moral codes, no basis for ethics. Man's uniqueness among social animals resides in the fact that his code of conduct is transmitted culturally rather than genetically. This is why man has a history and other species have palaeontology (fossil

*Monod, J., On values in the age of science, essay presented at the Fourteenth Nobel Symposium, 1969.

remains as evidence of their existence); hence the burden and the compulsive need for man to have a foundation, the ultimate justification for a set of values, for a code of ethics. This is what has provided the drive for religions and philosophies—to establish that source, that ultimate frame of reference for values. If science can demonstrate, however, that man's emergence is the outcome of a huge "Monte Carlo game", and that the Cosmos may not have even noticed nor cared about his emergence, then there is no ultimate source nor foundation for values or ethics outside of man himself. Man has, therefore, not only the need but also the freedom to create them, rather than to discover them.

The diversity of ideas and convictions about the origin, the nature, and the destiny of man led to the systematization of thoughts into sets of values and ideologies. Their formulation has, of course, also been influenced by the particular experiences of different societies, the physical environment that societies had to cope with, and, thus, the periods in which they emerged. The conflicts between ideologies are due more to the above (whence the differences about the past) than to fundamental differences in perceptions about the yearnings of man and the ultimately desirable things, and the societal order that could satisfy these yearnings.

Among the key "desirables" that man's mind focused on were his conditions of wealth and welfare, equality of opportunities or benefits, equality before law or in status and position, rights versus privileges, freedom and justice—both their source and their attainment.

Whatever man considers to be the desirable states or conditions, these can be attained only through interactions with people. What the nature of such interactions should be depends on how much importance is assigned to the individual in relation to the society. One of the systems of values that has emerged and that is strongly upheld in the Anglo-Saxon world assigns the primacy to the individual, his development, and his self-fulfilment. Whatever institutions are created should be so designed as to facilitate individual pursuits. This set of beliefs will be discussed under individualistic-competitive values in ch. 4.1.

Another body of beliefs sees man as very much a part of the societal fabric and sees the need for each individual to find his place in a societal structure, to play his particular role in it, to voluntarily subordinate himself to the societal needs. Such beliefs, characteristic of the Confucian and Shintoist cultures, have influenced strongly the behaviour of men in countries such as Japan. They will be explored further under the title of group-cooperative values.

Yet another way of seeing man is just as part of a community, inextricable from it. Man should fuse himself into communal existence. Such beliefs are being propagated in the Soviet Union and experimented with in China. This set of values can be labelled egalitarian-collectivist.

The different prescriptions and institutions that have emerged to regulate relations between men have links to one of the above three sets of values. The institutionalized interactions between men are of at least two different kinds: political and economic. The first category of interactions concerns the question of power. Power is the right, the capacity, to make decisions affecting whole communities. Among the key questions concerning power are: What justifies the right to use it? How is it acquired or how should it be acquired? Should it be concentrated or diffused? How can it be perpetuated or removed, constrained or controlled? The questions can also be formulated in terms of how and by whom laws can be passed, administered, and enforced; who can decide about taxes, pensions, or other resource allocations; how and by whom can decisions be made about war, peace, or, at the other end of the spectrum, about the manner of garbage collection. To be useful, an ideology needs to contain a set of prescriptions for the design of political institutions, which regulate the relationships of power between people and, through proper relationships, allow the attainment of political yearnings and aspirations.

The second set of interactions requiring some ideological prescriptions concerns physical goods and services—economic things. Given the existence of the physical needs of man, of those drives and yearnings that can be satisfied through material means, there has to be a system of production and distribution of wealth. Primitive man and his elemental family existed in the state of economic self-sufficiency. The desire to improve his lot has pushed man into the differentiation of productive roles, specialization of tasks, specialized production and exchange of goods, and has taken him through the stages of tribal, regional, national, and international organization to the currently complex economic institutions, which are interlinked and interdependent. Again, the economic experience of man varied depending on the conditions of natural endowment under which he lived, the degree of mastery over the physical environment that he attained, and the social and political organizations that facilitated or impeded the effectiveness of the economic processes. The economic purpose of an ideology, therefore, is to prescribe an effective or just economic system that would enable an efficient creation and/or equitable distribution of material goods. The economic component of the ideology has to provide answers to such problems as how to motivate man for productive effort, what should be the reward system, the ownership of the means of production, and the basis for allocation of exchange of goods.

Views have differed as to which of the two components of ideology, the political or the economic, should be the predominant one. Some, notably Marx, have held that economic factors determine other institutions in the social and political structure. Others place greater importance on political organization and consider it the component that determines the efficacy and justice of an economic system. Both historic and current observations show, though, that causality and determinism go in both directions. Thus the political governance can and does influence not only the shape but also the functioning of the economic system and vice versa, though it appears that the impact of the economic system on the political governance takes longer to materialize.

What is perhaps more important to observe is that these two components of the societal order, i.e. the political governance and the economic system, exist in various combinations. This being the case, they clearly do not fully determine each other. They can be decoupled, disconnected, "crossbred", and recombined to permit the creation of new societal designs or blueprints that show ways for societies to evolve to more desirable conditions.

But first we must discuss in more detail the three sets of values, the main variants of political governance, and the economic systems that have been the constituent elements of ideologies and the main components of ensuing societal orders.

CHAPTER 4

The Components of Societal Orders

Values

Since we are interested in the effectiveness of societies, it is those value/beliefs that influence the relationships between individuals or groups, the relationships within the whole society as such, that are of focal interest. The most useful way of categorizing values, therefore, is according to the degree of importance assigned to self, others, or the community as a whole, thus: individualistic-competitive, group-cooperative, or egalitarian-collectivist.

In some countries core values are clear and broadly shared; in others they are more pluralistic. Within most nation-states, however, there is a predominant set of beliefs either applied or at least postulated.

INDIVIDUALISTIC-COMPETITIVE

The origins of individualistic-competitive values can be traced to religious beliefs, to particular societal experiences, and historically abundant physical environments. Their perpetuation has been facilitated by the absence of imminent common external threats. Following is a brief analysis of the evolution of this set of values.

According to some religions (e.g. Christianity), man has been created in the image of God as a unique creation, above all others, predestined for mastery over others. Each individual, being an autonomous entity, can legitimately focus on self, both to fulfil his temporal needs and aspirations and to seek his spiritual salvation. Focal objectives for man's existence are, thus, the fulfilment of himself and the securing of his hereafter. Both of these objectives can only be attained through individual effort and merit. To satisfy his temporal needs and aspirations, he has to apply an intensive effort. To assure his here-after, man has to struggle against temptations, avoid evil, and do good. In both cases he must strive, but he has the freedom to decide how hard he tries. Differential effort, therefore, should be awarded, accordingly, differentially. On the scales of rewards and punishments there are sainthood and/or serenity versus damnation and, in the temporal life, wealth and comfort versus failure, poverty, and misery. Differentiation in rewards for effort induces and justifies the competi-tion for rewards. Success in any pursuit is measured in terms of success of others; in comparison to others, it is achieved in competi-tion with others. There are winners and losers.

One should feel compassion for the losers, demonstrate generosity to the less fortunate, less aspiring, less energetic, less achieving, but one should continue to do one's best to accomplish and to excel. The communal good is a by-product of individual self-fulfilment pursuits. Society should be so structured as to facilitate individual pursuits and to serve the interests of individuals, and, therefore, should be subordinate to individuals.

There may have been some distortions of the Divine Intention in this interpretation, but it suited man's instinctive inclinations. This view was further reinforced and justified when man found himself in an environment that was abundant and rich—such as that of the early American nation in 1776. There was space for each individual to move about without constraining others; many virgin lands to domesticate and to convert into private property through individual effort, without necessarily depriving others of such opportunities. One had to strike out on one's own and depend on one's own forces and resources. Distant authorities could not be of much help, so they could neither prescribe nor constrain too much. There was need for some mutual help, but there were also some clashes of will whenever interests conflicted or serious attempts to constrain were made. The above situation moulded and upheld characteristics of behaviour such as rugged individualism, self-reliance, pragmatism, mobility, nonconformism, ambition, achievement, drive, and competitiveness.

There was another factor favouring the development of this indi-vidualistic value system. It was the preselection of people who were individualistically inclined before they arrived in the USA. Some brought with them the British heritage of striving for individual freedoms and self-assertion, favoured by the absence of external security threats to the nation. Most were people escaping from essentially feudal societies, in which they felt economically exploited, religiously discriminated against, or politically constrained. They felt stifled under the wet blankets of old societal orders. They were predisposed, therefore, to individualistic beliefs and behaviour, and were determined to prove the merits of their beliefs.

In the abundant environment, individual success tended also to be largely beneficial to the new community at large. Even when the pioneering phase was followed by technological triumphalism, a single man's invention not only brought wealth to him but also amplified the potential of multitudes. In the eighteenth and nineteenth centuries the influence of the dominant religion, the self-selection of self-assertive people, and the abundant physical environment converged and reinforced each other, shaping and focusing to the extreme a set of individualistic values.

Are these determinants of values still valid? The interpretation of the dominant protestant–fundamentalist religion in the United States may have been a particular one, perhaps somewhat at variance with the will of the Creator. It may have focused unduly on man as an individual rather than on man as a part of humanity. It is, therefore, subject to review. The memories of the constraining societal orders from which the immigrants came were at times distorted and with time faded. Within a couple of generations the balance in the physical environment shifted from overabundance to a shortage of some resources, from unlimited elbow room to urban and highway congestion, from epic journeys requiring inordinate individual efforts, resourcefulness, and occasional violence to an hour's flight by jet; all of this thanks to the organized cooperative effort of many thousands. The society went from frontier "law", enforced at the end of a gun, to a multitude of laws passed within a single year by various legislatures, which if piled up in a single stack of paper would be several feet high. A very quick transition from a "cowboy" to a "spaceship" world.

Given some loss of influence of the dominant religion and some reinterpretation of it, the receding memories of the pioneering days, the "shrinkage" of the physical world, and constraining international interdependence, can the highly individualistic-competitive values continue to provide the guidelines for effective, functional behaviour of individuals and for the design of institutions that, in turn, would perpetuate such behaviour?

GROUP-COOPERATIVE

The key tenets of this set of values are as follows: man is only part—but an integral part—of creation. He should be in harmony, in symbiosis with nature and particularly with other people. Man is endowed with unique features, but not predestined nor expected to be master of all other things. Since man is just a component part of humanity and society, the meaning of his existence and his destiny are rooted in the society. His links to it are many: his immediate family, the extended family spanning those of the past and those yet to come, his work group, his company, the wider community, his nation. Good functioning of these various entities has primacy over the individual's needs and desires.

Each individual has a special role, but more as a thread in the societal fabric than apart from it or in opposition to it. Therefore each must fit into the societal fabric so that it can function well. Man has to live up to his societal obligations. He should subordinate himself voluntarily to group or societal objectives that exist in certain hierarchies, e.g. nation, company, work team or family—though not necessarily in that order.

Man's worth is assessed more in terms of his willingness and ability to live up to expectations than by his excelling over others. Virtue lies, therefore, in the domination over self rather than in the exteriorization of self, in conforming to expectations rather than in individualistic self-assertion and differentiation.

Given these beliefs, the resultant behaviour is more group than individually oriented, more cooperative than competitive, the relations between individuals based more on mutual obligations and loyalty than on mutual advantage and contractual agreements.

The roots of these values can be traced back to religious and mystic interpretations of the origin, nature, and destiny of man. Such values were further moulded by man's experience in coping with specific, tight, austere physical environments and, in some cases, by the external, hostile, political world. Among the countries with predominantly group-cooperative values, Japan is the one where the origins of such values can be most readily understood. For the sake of comparison with the United States we can again go back to 1776, but this time to Japan. The main religion, Shintoism, being polytheistic, favoured the above interpretation of the place of the individual in the universe and society. If one accepts the notion of many gods, it is much easier to accept the notion that man is just a part of creation and not a unique one, a part of society rather than a strictly individual entity. The physical environment enhanced the wisdom and utility of such an interpretation and gave credence to it. The islands were relatively small, already with many people. Much of the space was taken up by mountains that offered little. There was limited space in which to manoeuvre without muscling in or pushing others aside. There were no real commons left to which to apply individual effort and to convert to private property. Fertile land was scarce. The most sensible way of surviving was the cultivation of rice. Production of rice, though, required terracing and irrigation. The first could be better done through cooperative effort, the second simply demanded it—even after the building of irrigation canals the water had to be shared.

The existing societal order of landlords (*daimyo*), warriors (*samurai*), peasants, and tradesmen, with well-defined roles, interdependencies, and strong loyalites, was both the reflection of group-cooperative beliefs and, partly, their source. The fact that Japan had existed by then for over a century and a half in almost perfect isolation from the rest of the world made the culture, and thus the values, highly homogeneous, strongly rooted, and shared by the bulk of the society.

It is surprising, perhaps, to observe that the values which developed in such special circumstances survived modernization (which started in 1868—Meiji Restoration), economic and imperialist expansion between the two world wars, the crushing defeat in the Second World War, and even the subsequent extraordinary economic growth, the conquest of world markets, and the accession to the club of economic giants. Manifestations of the dominant group-cooperative values abound at different levels of contemporary Japanese society. "Japan Incorporated" can exist because of it. The "economic string quartet" (MITI, banks, trading houses, group companies) functions in accordance with it. The resuscitation of the officially dismantled Zaibatsu (the Japanese-type conglomerates) is explainable by it. These values also underlie the "bottom-up" style of management, with lifelong employment, a seniority system, group responsibility, conflict avoidance, search for consensus and mutual loyalty as the main foundations of relationships between people. All of these are realities; they determine the behaviour of the people; they have facilitated their recent accomplishments.

The Japanese did not launder out of themselves individual ambitions, drives, inclinations, and yearnings. They just tried to domesticate such sentiments and search for their fulfilment through playing their proper roles in the societal structure. There is much evidence that these other drives exist. For example, there is strong competition between firms within Japan, except when the national good dictates otherwise; strong competition with the rest of the world, where national good clearly demands it; occasional individual breakthroughs in technical innovations, and in the setting up of new corporations and organizations. There are also the occasional violent demonstrations, since self-discipline and voluntary subordination appear, to some members of the community, to be too high a price to pay for the smooth functioning of the societal fabric.

These pressure-release valves fulfil a tranquillizing function for the more assertive, restless members of the society, while the majority continues to conform to the norms of what is considered to be socially good and expected behaviour.

Serious questions arise about the survival of the values described above. Japan has opened up to the world. It opened itself to massive importation of goods and knowledge of all kinds from individually oriented societies. It exposed itself to alternate, even competing, values that can now be propagated effectively thanks to modern communication means, of which the Japanese produce more than their share. There has been quick urbanization and, hence, detachment from a nature that, in an earlier period, had imposed its stern demands. The Japanese family has shrunk from the extended one spanning several generations to its present atomic size consisting of parents and children. While all this would indicate that the battle for survival of the group-cooperative values will be a tough one, it will not necessarily be a losing one. Japan is only one example of several oriental cultures—and nations—that have been exposed to similar religious and cultural influences, have lived in similar physical environments, and now manifest some similarity in beliefs and behaviour. All belong to the Sino-Confucian zone. They are: Formosa, Singapore (with its predominant Chinese population), and South Korea. All of them have demonstrated in recent decades a great deal of vitality. They have been extraordinarily successful in absorbing technical knowledge from other parts of the world, and all have achieved significant rates of economic development. The above accomplishments have been realized in spite of (or, probably, because of) the retention of many traditional values and social schemes, while importing, wholesale, technical know-how from the Western world.

While Japan and some other Asian countries are the real bastions of group- or family-oriented, cooperative, supportive behaviour, we also find some predisposition to voluntary discipline and cooperation elsewhere—even among Western, "Hellenic"-culture countries like Germany or Sweden. The motives, the basis for relationships, and institutional arrangements are different, but some of the effects are the same (i.e. better mobilization and harmonization of individual efforts than one currently finds in extremely individualistic societies).

The test of the viability of group-cooperative values will lie in their continued utility as guidelines for coping with the contemporary and future physical environment and for maintaining effective interaction with societies based on different beliefs. Since spaces and resources are shrinking, since interdependence is increasing, cooperative predispositions seem of the essence. The only question is: Will nations with such values be able to transcend their group and national loyalties and egoisms, and become constructive partners in a world order?

EGALITARIAN-COLLECTIVIST

All of the value systems recognize man as an individual with attributes and characteristics that distinguish him from others. All of them, also, recognize that much of the meaning of man's existence is derived from interaction with others. Where the value systems differ is in how much emphasis they give to man as an individual or to man as a member of a community and, thus, to the nature and importance of his interaction with others. Individualistic-competitive values assert that it is man as an individual, his differentiation and self-seeking, that matters most. In group-cooperative values, the dominant thought is the willing subordination of individuals to the communal good. In the egalitarian-collectivist set of values, preponderant weight is given to man as a member of a community, his interaction with others, and, almost, his fusing into a collective entity.

Collectivist ideas and ideals have roots in some religious beliefs, some ethical and philanthropic motives, but are defined most clearly in Marxist doctrines. Concrete manifestations of these ideals span different historical periods, from early societies through contemporary states to blueprints for future societal orders. The key ideas are the following: man is born equal, not just in terms of equality of opportunity or equality before the law, but also equality of rights for the satisfaction of his needs. The cardinal prescription is, therefore, "to each according to his needs", but the necessary precondition for this (thus the first part of the cardinal rule) is "from each according to his ability".

The origin of collectivist ideals has often been ascribed to their roots in religions; but different interpretations of religious doctrines can result in almost diametrically opposing conclusions. One can interpret Christianity, for instance, in the following ways: man has been created in the image of God, therefore, as a unique being. This emphasis on man as an individual provides the legitimacy for focusing on self. On the other hand, one can stress that other men have been created in the image of God as well. Therefore, all men are equal before the Creator. Given prescriptions such as "love thy neighbour as thyself" or "do unto others as you wish others to do unto you", man can be seen as only a part of the human community. The essence of his existence, then, lies in sharing with others. From there it is only one step to the ideal of communal ownership and living. The ethical and philanthropic grounds for communal existence are related also to the above thinking.

A very different reasoning in favour of the egalitarian-collectivist society, and one that has had much greater mobilizing power in recent history, is rooted in scientific materialism, which sees man as a product of evolution, governed by natural laws of evolution. In short, the Marxist school of thought.

Marxism offers a historic analysis and predictions/prescriptions for the future: man has been motivated in the past by his economic self-interest because he lived under conditions of material scarcity. Similarity of interests made people bond into social classes. These classes were in conflict with each other because of differences in their economic interests, e.g. owners versus workers. Owners of the means of production will keep expanding their facilities and minimizing wages in order to enrich themselves. The expansion of the means of production will lead to competitive struggles for markets and to diminishing returns and a weakening of the system—but, at the same time, to the numerical expansion of the impoverished proletariat. As they grow conscious of their numerical strength, the proletariat will overthrow the weakening capitalist class and create a rational system for production and distribution of goods. This will allow the creation of a base for material affluence and the possibility to satisfy the material needs of the whole population. Once these conditions are achieved and scarcity—the previous determinant of human behaviour—abolished, the behaviour of people should alter radically from individualistic-competitive to cooperative-supportive. The state of communism can then be introduced, based on the principle "to each according to his needs and from each according to his ability", since there will be no need to fight over scarce resources. Class differences and, therefore, conflicts, will disappear, and the state apparatus previously required to regulate such conflicts could wither away.

In different periods of history there have been various attempts to apply in practice egalitarian-collectivist values. In early societies there were forms of primitive communism, particularly in island communities. For instance, sea fishing required some organized group effort, cooperation, and apportioning of the catch for the survival of the community. Thus developed ways of sharing both the effort and the product. According to anthropologists, sharing was not based on the principle "to each according to his needs", but on a system of entitlements, such as relationship to the fisherman, role performed in the community, etc. In predominantly pastoral societies, communal rather than individual ownership of pastures seemed eminently sensible. This reduced the labour required, facilitated the rational use of pastures, and permitted the nomadic existence of collective moves to greener pastures. The emphasis in this form of societal organization, however, was put on collective use of property and cooperative effort rather than on subsequent sharing of the fruits of the effort.

The attempts in the early nineteenth century in the United Kingdom and the United States to create egalitarian-collectivist forms of organization were largely inspired by religious, ethical, and philanthropic motives. Some communities were organized along communist lines. They were out of tune with the dominant values in their societies and were viewed by contemporaries as Utopian experiments, and, thus, they failed. The more recent experiments with communal living in the United States, including the extreme forms of sharing such as communal sex, have also largely failed, again because they were too much out of tune with the dominant values of the ambient society.

Another interesting example of the practice of the egalitarian-collectivist philosophy is the kibbutzim in Israel. They were partly Marxist inspired and partly patriotically motivated. The purpose was to settle land and produce some food within the country. While there remains some of the initial motivation, enough members must have found sufficient satisfaction in this form of organization and life style to wish to continue, regardless of patriotic imperatives. The kibbutz is a rather extreme form of collectivism. There is no private ownership, everything belongs to the collective, and members have equal rights to participate in the decisions. The prescription "to each according to his needs and from each according to his ability" is largely applied. What is particularly interesting is that this form of organization exists at the subsocietal level and, in fact, in fairly sharp contrast to the ways in which much of the rest of the industry, commerce, and even the political life of the country are organized. They are like egalitarian-collectivist islands in an individualistic-competitive sea.

The most significant developments and experiences have been rooted in Marxist philosophy. The October 1917 Revolution was fought and won under its banner; the Czarist Russian Empire was transformed into the Soviet Union, currently one of the most powerful countries. The most populous nation in the world, China, also went through a social revolution, using a Marxist vision of the future as a mobilizing force and a societal blueprint. Other smaller countries, in various ways, have gone into the egalitarian-collectivist camp. A third of humanity, therefore, now has Marxism, in its diverse interpretations, as an official ideology.

None of the countries concerned proclaims to have reached the stage of full communism. Some, like China, feel that they are close to the ideal, since they have a relatively high equality in the distribution of wealth and in standards of living, even though at a low level of prosperity. Others are resolutely in the transient stage, the function of which is to build affluence and, thus, prepare the material basis for introducing communism. During this transitory stage, inequalities are allowed and differential rewards for differential effort are given in order to motivate people for more productive pursuits. This should accelerate the creation of material affluence, still seen as a precondition for the introduction of true communism.

The egalitarian-collectivist set of values, like the preceding two, can be analysed in moral or utilitarian terms. The first way evokes such questions as: Has man really been predestined to a collectivist-type of existence, either by Divine Will or by the laws of nature? Is it sufficiently reflective of his true nature? Can it accommodate the observable uniqueness of each individual? The utilitarian "acid test" questions that suggest themselves are: Can egalitarian-collectivist forms of existence evoke the most creative, productive abilities of man, both by providing the motivation and the opportunity for creative effort? Can it, therefore, facilitate technological and economic progress? Can it, if not eliminate, at least significantly reduce conflicts within a society? Will man voluntarily share and voluntarily do his best for communal good? Can he be induced to do so through a new type of education or is there some compulsion required? Can one reach a discrete point on the scale of economic progress at which one can declare the state of affluence and then introduce true communism? Is not the notion of affluence a very relative one? Can satisfaction be derived from more cooperative interaction with other people, outweighing almost instinctive individual drives and yearnings, or is there a need to coerce man into such behaviour?

The appeal of egalitarian-collectivist values has obviously been widespread. Their mobilizing power has been great. Their feasibility has been tested, at least on a subsocietal scale such as in the kibbutzim. The industrial and military accomplishments in some countries mobilized around these ideas have been significant. The social and political costs that have accompanied such accomplishments are judged by most to have been excessive. In view of all the above, are these likely to be the values towards which the world of tomorrow will converge?

Political Governance

The second key component of any societal order is the totality of its political institutions and procedures, which we will name political governance. There are many ways of categorizing and describing the nature of political regimes varying in analytical rigour and utility. The most common political labels tend to have the greatest mobilizing power, but contribute little to true understanding since people attribute different meanings to them. They are more useful for creating or sustaining political tensions than as a basis for novel political architecture. A case in point is words like democracy versus autocracy.

The label autocratic is a derogatory one. It automatically evokes connotations like dictatorial, oppressive, arbitrary, unjust, usurpatory. No government chooses to label itself thusly.

In contrast to autocracy, democracy as a concept, an ideal, a desirable form of political governance has gained tremendously in popular appeal in recent history; it has an almost universal acceptance in the contemporary world. If this assertion sounds surprising, think of any current political regime that proclaims itself to be undemocratic or antidemocratic. Even those regimes that exercise absolute power justify it by using democratic terminology. Those who abrogate democratic institutions explain their actions as temporary expedients necessitated by special circumstances. This strong appeal, the almost hypnotic power of the word democratic, means that it strikes a resonant chord in people who reach a certain stage of political consciousness and maturity.

The term democracy, however, covers a number of distinctive variants of political governance that have existed in the past and exist today. The main ones are as follows.

Direct democracy. In this system, members of a given community take a direct part in the making of political decisions, such as passing laws or deciding on specific actions. A strong justification for it has been articulated by Jean-Jacques Rousseau: "No law is legitimate unless it is an expression of general will, a consensus of the whole community. No man can enjoy full moral responsibility, and so really be a man, unless he participates in the formation of the consensus, by which he is legally bound."*

Representative democracy. Members of a community still retain the ultimate source of authority and the right to make decisions, but they exercise that right through their elected representatives. The justification for this system has been more utilitarian than moral since, physically, it appeared too difficult to gather all members of a community in one place in order to have them take direct part in the making of laws or in the making of executive decisions. The system of electing representatives, who should act as spokesmen for their electorate and in the spirit of their will, offered a solution to this problem.

Constitutional democracy. Power is exercised by elected representatives, but they are constrained both in the making of laws and in their execution by a constitution prescribing boundaries of laws and powers, protecting the rights of minorities and individuals. The need for a constitution is broadly recognized, yet constitutions have been and are still sometimes used as a substitute for legality rather than a base for it.

Social or economic democracy. The avowed primary purpose is the reduction of social-economic differences rather than the assuring of equality of opportunities, equality before law, or ultimate individual

---

*Rousseau, J.-J., *Du Contrat Social*, first written in 1762, French & European Publications, New York, 1971.

freedoms. Direct involvement in economic decision-making by those involved in the productive processes is another key tenet.

Totalitarian democracy. This is the extreme incarnation of economic democracy. It is rooted in the proposition that the economic condition of man is the chief determinant of his political and social status. Economic equality is seen as a necessary precondition for political equality. The concentration of power in the hands of a dictator, an oligarchy, or a single party is justified in terms of social transformations necessary to bring about economic equality. The term democratic in this case is used to imply that power is exercised for the good of the people and, therefore, in the name of the people.

The above brief discussion of democracy shows the difficulty of using this conventional way of categorizing forms of political governance. The taxonomy: countervailing, shared, and unitary power seem to me more descriptive of how authority—the right to govern, to make decisions—is actually used. Most countries fall readily into one of these categories. The description of these three variants of political governance follows.

COUNTERVAILING POWERS

The countervailing power form of political governance is rooted in individualistic-competitive values and exists in countries where these values are dominant, such as the Anglo-Saxon, English-speaking countries. Its main characteristics are as follows: there are those in power and those in opposition; powers are normally divided along legislative, executive, and judiciary lines, and, especially in the American version, the institutions are so designed as to act as a system of checks and balances on each other.

This type of governance emerged mainly as a reaction to or evolution of unitary power. It may be useful to trace its evolution before analysing its essence. Unitary power types of governance vary in the degree of concentration of power from absolute authority vested in a single person to significant sharing of it with small groups within the society. Rome existed as an oligarchic republic in which a small proportion of the population had very extensive powers. It transformed itself into an autocratic empire. The medieval/feudal societies had in them some seeds of countervailing powers. Some monarchies, as in the United Kingdom, were not absolute, since the monarchs depended on the consent of feudal lords, ecclesiastic authorities, and chartered cities for such things as taxes. Gatherings of these bodies to agree on new taxes and other major decisions were the precursors to modern parliaments. Monarchies were not only limited in the use of power by the above, but also by the need to maintain the legitimacy of their power. The legitimacy could have three possible roots: Divine Will, bestowing some authority upon the monarch; the so-called "natural reason"; and the conformance of the exercise of power to the "law of the land", a set of beliefs and conventions that evolved over time about what was right or wrong. Constitutions emerged in the attempt to codify what was right or wrong, what the law of the land was, and to put limits on the exercise of power to protect certain inviolable rights.

While in the sixteenth and seventeenth centuries the absolute sovereignties reasserted themselves, the powers of absolute monarchs were broken again, in some countries through revolutions, in others through gradual evolution. The parliaments gained in power. In the United Kingdom, parliament first acquired the right to legislate, to decide on financial matters, and then asserted its supremacy over the executive branch of the government. The ensuing separation between the legislative and executive powers, for which John Locke provided the philosophical foundation (*Of Civil Government*),* started giving a clear shape to the countervailing powers type of governance. The ideas about the separation of powers, including the judiciary as an autonomous entity, were elaborated on and popularized by Baron de Montesquieu (*The Spirit of Laws*).† This separation remains a foundation stone of the Anglo-Saxon models of contemporary, democratic, types of government.

The concept of separation of powers is based on the assumption that man is fallible and may be predisposed to do evil. The institu-

---

*Locke, J., *Of Civil Government 2nd Essay*, first written in 1690, Regenry-Gateway, South Bend, Indiana, 1960.

†Baron de Montesquieu, *The Spirit of Laws*, first written in 1735–40, University of California Press, California, 1978.

tions must be designed to guard against man's fallibility. This kind of thinking provided the justification for the emergence of opposition, another true milestone in the development of political governance institutions. To assure that parliament passed laws that were just and that the government executed them justly, an opposition had to exercise the power of restraint, of counterweight, both in the legislative process and in the executive function (calling the government to order, a vote of no confidence, etc.).

While men design institutions, the shape of the institutions influences the behaviour of men. Thus, if the sole purpose of the opposition were to moderate the use of power by those who exercise it, the role could be played constructively and loyally. If limited to this role, however, the motivation to assume it would diminish with time. The system, therefore, provides for periodic elections. The rationale for them is eminently sound:

—to assure that government (legislative and executive branches) remains representative of the will of the majority;
—to stimulate good performance by those in power by promise of ultimate reward through reelection;
—to prevent the abuses of power that can stem from unduly prolonged use of it, thus the ultimate punishment of non-reelection (American and British schoolchildren are reminded almost daily of Lord Acton's statement: "Power tends to corrupt and absolute power corrupts absolutely");*
—to sustain the motivation of the opposition by the prospect of accession to power.

It is this last point that seems vital and yet in practice can lead to distortions and even to some "degeneration" of the system. As long as the focal purpose of the opposition would be to moderate the use of power, the system could function well. When, however, the dominant motive (naturally enough) becomes to accede to power, then the ensuing behaviour can become somewhat perverse; the purpose of opposition becomes to oppose. This leads to attempts to diminish those in power, to sharpening of differences, amplification of conflicts, polarization of societal forces, increase of frictions, and, thus, conver-

*Lord Acton, Letter to Bishop Mandell Creighton, 5 April 1887.

sion of potentially useful societal energies into waste political heat. This process can justifiably be termed social–political entropy. At the limit, it becomes an institutionalized, legitimate, and even virtuous destruction of power (i.e. the capacity to do, to accomplish).

The particular processes have become readily observable: to be elected, one has to appeal to the electorate. The easiest way of doing this is by criticizing those in power for their ineffectiveness, ineptness, dishonesty, corruption, and viciousness, and, on the other hand, to promise to "deliver" what the electorate desires and "deserves" through better programmes, greater integrity, more effective organization, better administration. The self-generating pressure is to exaggerate, to bid higher, to raise the aspirations and expectations of the population. The system becomes a political stock exchange in which power can go to the highest bidder. When the opposition gets into power, the roles get reversed, but the process continues. To satisfy the expectations is more difficult than to generate them. Therefore, there are disappointments, increased pressures on those in power, etc. To stay in power one has to keep up the popularity poll. The resulting actions become motivated more by the desire to win the forthcoming elections than by the ultimate societal good. The time horizon in political decision-making becomes shorter. The longer-term consequences become underestimated, rational remedies less applicable, and key problems can remain unsolved. The recent inability to cope with inflation in societies in which popularity is the *sine qua non* of staying in power is very eloquent in this respect.

Periodic elections were also intended to act as antidotes to "corruption of power", sort of political menstrual cycles, a way of cleansing the systems out. But this causes discontinuities, sometimes reversals of policies, and again waste of energies and a slowdown of societal progress.

There are other features in the countervailing powers type of governance that are questionable. In some, the majority rule means that sizeable minorities can be imposed upon, legally coerced. Such minorities can lose the feeling of having a stake in the society, become alienated from it, and can react in a destructive fashion, such as massive strikes or even violence. On the other hand, laws and institutions that are intended to provide full protection of minorities can give the well-organized, articulate minorities a disproportionate amount of influence over the legislative or executive processes. Those that are less organized, less rich, or less vocal, even if more numerous, can thus also become alienated.

There are even more important reasons for some fundamental rethinking of the system. There were several specific factors that helped shape the political institutions in the United Kingdom and the United States. First, there were religious differences. In order for them not to erupt into Continental European-type religious wars, ways of accommodating the differences, some checks, and balances, had to be found.

The absence of real external threats to the countries made it possible to spend more energy on debating internal issues. On the other hand, the challenge of expanding the empire in the United Kingdom and of domesticating the rich continent in the United States provided enough mobilizing power and cohesion to paste over some strains provoked by internal power games. The increasing wealth in both countries made the political games an affordable luxury.

The above conditions have changed radically in recent years. Religious differences in those countries are not of the essence; some ethnic, racial, and social ones are more important now, requiring different modes of conflict resolution. The empire has vanished, as have the open rich spaces. The prosperity and the good functioning of countries calls for a closing of the ranks; the stock exchange of political promises makes it difficult to do so, though. Self-restraint and self-discipline, required in view of shortages and external limits to manoeuvre, are not natural by-products of governance by Gallup poll.

SHARED-CONSENSUAL POWER

There are two distinctive variants of the shared-consensual form of political governance in which institutions and processes of decision-making are very different yet the final results are the same. Both lead to a high degree of consensus in their respective societies with an absence of sharp divisions or conflicts, and disciplined adherence to and rather effective implementation of decisions and policies.

The best example of the first variant is the case of Switzerland. This type of governance coexists with individualistic-competitive values because there is both formal sharing of power through permanent coalitions at all levels of political governance in that society and, at the same time, there exists direct democracy with very frequent participation of the population in the taking of concrete decisions, again at the various levels of political organization, going from federal through cantonal down to communal.

The Swiss type of direct democracy has historical antecedents. A form of direct democracy existed in some primitive societies where members of the community took a direct part in the decision-making process. Such practices were limited to communities of relatively small size. A similar system was developed and practised in a much more sophisticated fashion in the Greek city-states, like Athens. While much more developed in methods and institutional forms, it was in some ways a retrogression from earlier forms of direct democracy since the right to participate in it was limited to citizens with the exclusion of slaves. Thus, again, the total numbers involved in the process were relatively small and the system presupposed a slave type of economy in order to allow the citizens the leisure to attend to civic matters. The attempts to extend the system from a single city-state and to create a bigger political entity similar to a modern nation-state, by applying a concept of confederation, failed completely. There were several causes for such failures. The communities concerned may not have been sufficiently compatible in the nature of their political experiences. Some feel that direct democracy can only function in relatively small communities. The contemporary experience of Switzerland does show, however, that it can function in a bigger entity like a nation-state.

What necessitated and facilitated the development of institutions for formal sharing of power through permanent coalitions of different parties in Switzerland is the fact that the Swiss Confederation has been built gradually over a long period of time, with new areas, now cantons, joining the Confederation mostly on a voluntary basis. Since such new areas had significant regional or language differences, they could only join the Confederation if they felt secure about the preservation of some of their differences. This presupposed that they would have a great deal of autonomy and some say in the governance of the whole Confederation.

Some of the principles of Swiss democracy and its institutional features have been described in the section on Western Europe. It may be useful to recall a few of the cornerstones of the philosophy concerning the sharing of power. It holds that the interest of individuals can best be served when they have the greatest possible opportunity to influence directly political decisions. Secondly, the more an individual can influence decisions, the more responsible he will feel towards the society as a whole. Therefore, the responsibility of each individual's behaviour towards the system as such depends primarily on his capacity to influence the system. From this, one derives the further relationship that broad diffusion and decentralization of power does not diminish the capacity of a society to do things, to accomplish them, or to mobilize itself, but, on the contrary, it will generate a greater commitment of citizens toward the society, hence amplifying the societal mobilizing capacity.

The second type of governance, more appropriately called consensual rather than shared power, functions not because the political institutions are designed that way, but because the underlying set of group-cooperative values creates a general predisposition in the population to avoid conflicts and to seek consensus. Japan is the best example of this form of governance, with its broad consultations and consensus-building constituting dominant features of the decision-making process.

Until the Second World War, Japan had a unitary power system. It varied in form from an absolute monarchy through an oligarchy to a constitutional monarchy. In the period of golden isolation (1602–1867) shoguns played a dominant role, but shared some power with the landlords (*daimyos*). Subsequently, there was a constitutional monarchy, which in reality was an oligarchy with power shared between the monarch and a small military and industrial élite. After the Second World War a new political system was inspired and designed by the Americans and readily accepted by the Japanese. Its main features are those of a constitutional monarchy, with the monarch reduced to a strictly symbolic role, and a parliamentary democracy with several political parties. The one that wins the majority of votes forms the government. In principle, therefore, there is the rule of the majority with opposition parties—in short, a classic set of countervailing power political institutions.

Transcending the above formal political structure, however, is consensus-building as the dominant process of political decision-making. It permeates the whole life of Japan. Group-cooperative values still largely determine the behaviour of the Japanese. There are some deeply rooted feelings that facilitate the process of consensus-seeking. First, there is the importance of face-saving, the dread of loss of face. This leads to the avoidance of direct confrontations of ideas, views, or alternatives. At various levels in the society, long discussions take place in order to develop a common understanding of a problem or situation and, thus, to find a solution as a natural by-product of such an understanding, rather than jumping quickly to alternative, competing proposals. Secondly, there is the willingness of individuals to subordinate themselves to higher purposes. Their views, suggestions, and actions can be fairly readily trusted since they are likely to be motivated at least partly by consideration of the good of a work group, a company, or the country.

The rapid postwar reconstruction, the three decades of extraordinary economic growth, and the successful coping with the aftermaths of such shocks as the petroleum crisis, testify to the efficacy of this system. Elections are contested and fought, parliamentary debates are genuine, and political manifestations not infrequent, but the strength of cultural traditions and values is such as to transcend such divisive forces and maintain a large degree of agreement and commitment at various levels of Japanese society.

There are countries, like Germany, whose political governance system falls between the two types described above. There is overt and direct competition for power among the political parties. If governments tend to be partial coalitions, it is because a single party cannot get a clear majority. There is no recourse to direct democracy in the decision-making processes. Yet there are some characteristics of a shared power system because of the integration of various sectors of the population, and particularly labour, into the political system, a reasonable degree of decentralization of power to the constituent states, sharing of power at the enterprise level, and, generally, "partnership" rather than adversarial relations between various social classes.

Switzerland, Japan, and Germany have been among the best "performing" countries during the last few decades. Other countries, particularly democracies of the Anglo-Saxon type, have difficulty, however, in extracting and transposing some of the useful lessons from these three societies.

The real nature of Swiss political institutions is either not sufficiently well known or the situation is dismissed as being something very special—a case of a small country with particularly mature people. Yet this governance system is not just an accident of geography. It has been carefully designed, incorporating some features of the American constitution, further tested, modified, and, above all, carefully and continuously nurtured. For the Swiss, power implies responsibility rather than privileges, and this has protected them from the corrosive effects of concentrated power.

Japan, while a big country, remains something of a mystery and is often more feared than admired. The extraordinary homogeneity of values is seen by many as being too unique to be of model value; yet, if we remember under what physical conditions those values have been distilled, this societal model does offer some learning potential for the future.

Germany, the undisputed economic champion in Europe, is still remembered for the ravages it caused. These were made possible by the predisposition to discipline and to some voluntary subordination; hence, a high mobilizing capacity, which can be misdirected. Yet, currently, the country performs well, not only on the economic front but also on the political. Some very useful lessons could be extracted from this particular societal experience.

UNITARY POWER

Unitary power covers a range of past and present political orders labelled absolute, autocratic, despotic, dictatorial, rightist or leftist, military or proletariat; other labels include one-party system, non-constitutional monarchies, revolutionary governments, tribal chiefdoms. In the contemporary world, most of the above descriptions have derogatory connotations. Present governments, even when exhibiting characteristics of a unitary power, describe themselves in different terms, using "democratic" as the predominant label. While the justification for the concentration of power varies, the fact of concentration is one of the common denominators of all the above variants.

Another common denominator is the absence of a legal opposition or counterweight and the difficulty for the population at large to take power away from those who exercise it and bestow it on others. In the past, such shifts in the locus of power could be effected only through violent means, such as a revolution, palace or popular, or a *coup d'état*—all such events often being facilitated by a defeat in war or other calamity or emergency.

How did unitary power governance emerge and why does it still survive? Any organization needs order, a set of rules to which members of the organization must conform. The source of such order and the ensuing rules are directly linked to ideas of man about his origin. Whether one feels that man is a product of Divine Will or a product of evolution governed by the laws of nature, the ultimate determining power and authority is outside and above man. It is, thus, very natural to perceive that there has to be an apex in any social organization, someone at the top of the power pyramid. It can be an absolute monarch who inherited his power from above, the head of "the true" church to whom the Creator revealed the truth, or it can be the "fittest" who survives the struggle among men, imposing the right of might as genuine tyrants do. But even when the dominant belief maintains that man has the right to self-determination, a unitary structure of power can arise as an expression of popular will. This happens when there is a sharp and shared perception of the need for a dramatic change in the societal and, mainly, economic order, as well as the conviction that such a societal transformation requires a strong hand, uninhibited by any dilution of power or by undue constraints.

If unitary power continues to have strong appeal, it is because it has some attractive features. It allows the creation and the pursuit of a unity of purpose. Priority can be given to national, collective, or communal needs over individual needs. It facilitates master planning and what appears to be a rational allocation of resources. It can enable quick decisions and fast implementation. Normally, it is an effective system for conduct of wars and for coping with other extreme emergencies.

This type of governance has some obvious disadvantages. It has engendered in the past, and continues to engender, passionate opposition. It then tends to eliminate all opposition to centralized power as such and to suppress any views not generated within the power structure. This leads to societal blinkers, with the ensuing danger of ignoring realities and moving off on tangents. Evolutionary progress is impeded: there is not enough competition of ideas, nor analysis of costs and benefits of different options, nor pragmatic adaptations to new realities. This system can allow those in power to become self-serving, arbitrary, or corrupt. The greatest single difficulty, though, is the need to impose the will of the leader, the party or the so-called "national will" on the people. This necessitates the creation of a supervising, controlling, and, usually, coercive bureaucracy that can stifle initiative, diminish motivation, and evoke more opposition.

One can make a fairly fundamental proposition at this stage: the effectiveness of authority or power is determined less by its intrinsic nature than by the degree to which it is voluntarily accepted by those over whom it is exercised, i.e.

$$\text{Effectiveness of power} = f \text{ (Acceptability of power)}$$

The conditions, therefore, under which concentrated authority—a unitary power form of governance—can be effective are as follows:

—when a community has no experience with or a full understanding of other systems;
—when people accept the authority of a single person or oligarchy for religious, moral, or expedience reasons;
—when a few are rich and the masses are poor;
—when a few are educated and the masses are ignorant;
—when a few are determined and the masses are apathetic, inert;
—when a few are aspiring and the masses are contented;
—in highly homogeneous cultures, in which values and wishes are shared by a great majority;

—in perceived external danger or emergency situations;

—when the promise of an improved future seems to outweigh the sacrifices (mainly individual freedoms) demanded by the unitary type of governance.

The unitary power type of governance will demonstrate ineffectiveness under the following conditions:

—when no sanctity is attributed to superior authority;

—when faced with economic interdependence rather than dependence of the poor on the rich;

—when the masses are educated;

—when the masses are politically conscious and energized;

—when many aspire to self-assertion;

—in heterogeneous, pluralistic countries;

—in the absence of imminent external threats to the society.

The above analysis abstracts from, but does not deny, the moral reasoning about the unitary power type of governance, i.e. whether the system conforms to the true nature, aspirations, and destiny of man. It may be useful, though, to analyse the question further in pragmatic, utilitarian terms, i.e: What is meant by effectiveness of political governance? It can be considered effective if it can maintain and perpetuate itself, if it facilitates technological and economic progress, if it satisfies the perceived needs of the bulk of the population. One can think of the effectiveness of a political power system in terms of energy balance. How much of the societal energy does it take to maintain the institutions of political governance? What is the output/input ratio? This in turn depends, as mentioned before, on how readily the bulk of the population accepts the authority of the unitary source of power, how readily it conforms to the prescribed behaviour. The more effort is required to assure acceptance, adherence, and subordination to the system, the more bureaucracy has to be built up, the greater the amount of energy that has to be diverted from economically or socially productive efforts to the maintenance of the power system itself. The energy wastage can create a vicious circle: the more coercion, the more dissatisfaction, the more opposition in various forms, the greater the menace to those in power, the greater the effort on their part to maintain themselves in power. Can such a vicious circle be broken without violent convulsions, without the revolutions that are so costly and so unpredictable in their final outcome?

Economic Systems

The third component of any societal order and an important determinant of any society's effectiveness is the economic system. Its functions are the production and distribution of wealth. The key issues within any economic system are what and how to produce, how to allocate, distribute or exchange, and whom and how to reward for a productive activity. The nature of any economic system depends on how the above issues are resolved. There are several distinctive prototype systems and various hybrid versions thereof. The key features of the "prototypes" are listed in Table 4.

The content of the table is a simplification of the reality; its sole purpose is to facilitate a quick comparison of these systems and to introduce an analysis of the conditions under which each of the systems can be most effective. Only the first three of the five prototypes have been mentioned in Chapter 1 (Effectiveness of Societies—An Overview), either because they exist in many countries or because the countries with such systems play important roles in the world economy. Two other prototypes are included here because one can extract useful lessons from them.

There are other possible ways of analysing and comparing economic systems. The descriptive features shown in Table 4 have been chosen because they have different ideological roots. They allow a comparison of the determinants of the efficacy of an economic system. The choice of labels for the five systems poses some problems. The commonly used labels like capitalism and communism have acquired, in many people's minds, purely derogatory connotations. Also, they are not sufficiently descriptive of current reality. Capitalism has undergone profound modifications such as disassociation between ownership and control of the means of production. The label "free enterprise", therefore, is felt to be more descriptive of the current

TABLE 4

Key features	Type of system				
	Free enterprise (capitalism)	Concerted free enterprise	Command-state enterprise	Distributive socialism	Market socialism
1. Main motive and/or performance criteria	Profit maximization	Growth and profit maximization	Output maximization	Profit	Viability
2. Nature of ownership	Private	Private	State	Private	Collective
3. Nature of market	Free	Free	Administered	Free	Controlled
4. Role of government	Limited to ascertaining above	To harmonize economic activities	Deciding; planning; controlling	To offset distributive injustices	Setting objectives; coordinating; regulating
5. Original rationale and main purpose	Economic; efficient production	Economic and political; enhancing position of nation. satisfaction of individual needs	Political; creating material base for communism	Social; efficient production; equitable distribution	Socio-Political; economic democracy through self-management

nature of this type of system since relative freedom of the markets and freedom to initiate new activities are its most characteristic features. "Concerted free enterprise", while closely resembling "free enterprise", deserves to be singled out because of the degree of harmonization of economic decisions, which is possible within countries where there is some subordination of private goals to national good.

Communism is not a good label for an economic system since it is more of an objective than a reality. The Soviet economy, which would fall into this category, is officially called a socialist economy. It is, however, a transient brand of socialism, an intermediary type of system whose main function is to prepare a base of material affluence for the introduction of communism. The label "command-state enterprise" reflects better both how the economic decisions are made and the ownership pattern.

"Distributive socialism", as applied for instance to Sweden, is an apt label. Its main thrust and purpose, as perceived by the socialist government for four decades, was justice in the distribution of wealth. "Market socialism", a label that has been applied to the case of Yugoslavia, may imply greater freedom of markets than actually exists there, but it highlights this feature, distinguishing the system from that of the Soviet Union, for example. The crucial characteristic of market socialism is the degree of workers' participation in the decision-making in the conduct of enterprises.

FREE ENTERPRISE

Capitalism succeeded the medieval, feudal systems whose main features were serfdom-based agricultures, artisanal production of nonagricultural goods, and a small commercial-service sector linking the first two. The society consisted of a few very wealthy and a great majority of very poor people. The wealthy ones excelled in conspicuous consumption rather than in productive investments of accumulated surpluses. There was, therefore, little improvement of productivity, little expansion of productive capacities, and little economic growth.

In a later period, several forces ushered in and moulded the shape of "capitalism". The expansion of foreign trade created the need for specialization, for increase in the size of production units, for commercial techniques and credit instruments, and, thus, aggregation of capital and its investment. Technical innovations permitted specialization and larger-scale manufacturing. The energies necessary for productive efforts were released and better mobilized by the Reformation and the emergence of the protestant ethic, which legitimized and encouraged the capitalist type of behaviour by showing an alternate road to salvation through hard work, frugality, and efficiency. The indulgence of wealth ceased to be the main purpose for its creation. The efficiency in its use became more important. This provided the moral justification for accumulation of wealth since, by definition, it would end up in the hands of the most efficient, thus the most virtuous. By stressing the sanctity of all work, the protestant ethic provided the motivation for dedicated, disciplined work at all levels of society.

Nation-states have helped in the subsequent development of "capitalism" by creating legal and institutional infrastructures such as legal codes, stable currencies, and domestic markets, and by assisting in the improvement and expansion of physical infrastructures such as transportation and communication. Thus they have helped fructify subsequent private investments in directly productive industrial and commercial activities.

Adam Smith, in his *Enquiry into the Nature and Causes of the Wealth of Nations* (1776), explained some of the observable features of capitalism, justified it mostly in economic but partly in moral terms, and gave it intellectual and ideological legitimacy, thereby facilitating its further development.

Further technological innovations and changes brought about the industrial revolution, with its mechanization, increased specialization, growth in productivity and sizes of enterprises, and drive for the expansion of markets.

Capitalism evoked many criticisms. The most fundamental challenge came from Karl Marx. He recognized that capitalism created massive productive forces in a relatively short period of time. He felt that it was a necessary phase for humanity to go through in order to break up previous, less-productive systems. But he thought that the system was terribly unjust and suffered from tensions and conflicts. Therefore it would inevitably collapse and, in its place, communism would be ushered in as the ultimate effective and just order.

In addition to the Marxist challenge and various movements engendered by it, capitalism had to go through other survival tests. In the process it evolved into what can now be more appropriately called "free enterprise". Among these further challenges were:

—loss of Western European leadership on the world scene, which shook the capitalist foundations in that part of the world;
—the great depression with its bankruptcies, renunciation of debts, reduction of foreign trade, and shaking up of monetary solidity and solidarity;
—Roosevelt's New Deal and the spread of the use of fiscal and monetary interventionism in the United States, the very country that had become the new bastion of capitalism;
—gradual diffusion of ownership of productive means through shareholding and the consequent separation of ownership from control.

The most serious threat was the birth and development of a radically different economic model, the command-state enterprise, as the result of the 1917 October Revolution.

Strong criticisms of the free enterprise system continue to come from within the countries committed to the system. The separation of ownership and management, already mentioned, creates the situation of "property without power and power without property", diminishing the original justification of power rooted in property as a "natural right". Resource scarcities, and shifting control over them, created constraints on economic growth, considered crucial for the viability of free enterprise.

All of the above challenges and threats have been the forces of change that together determined the direction of evolution of free enterprise economies. Given the above historical background, we can now examine the nature of that evolution and the transformations that the system in question has undergone. This will be done by reviewing its original design features, the problems stemming from them and criticisms levelled at them, then the reactions, corrective actions, and reforms. This evolution is summarized in Table 5.

TABLE 5. *Evolution of the free enterprise system*

Key features	Ensuing problems and criticisms	Reactions and reforms
1. *Maximization of profits* to create surpluses; investment; growth	Overexpansion; minimization of wages; impoverishment of the proletariat	Emergence of trade unions; minimum wage legislation; reduction of poverty
2. *Private ownership* A "natural right" and reward of the efficient	Possibility to accumulate wealth in fewer hands	Progressive income and inheritance taxes; spread and institutionalization of ownership
3. *Free markets* competition directs factors of production to the most efficient	Free market leads to cyclical variations, depressions, monopolization, cartels, underemployment of resources	Fiscal, monetary, and other interventions; antitrust legislation; some price controls
4. *Limited role of government* Individual pursuit of self-interest will assure satisfaction of greatest number	Permits material and other inequalities; favours individual over public consumption needs; allows high unemployment	Social legislation: old-age pension, health and unemployment insurance; public works; multiplication of controls
5. *Original purpose* efficient production of wealth and satisfaction of individuals' needs	Economic and social injustices	Social and political criteria gradually incorporated into decision-making and evaluation of performance of enterprises

Profit maximization is an important motive of a private enterprise and the main criterion by which its effectiveness is judged. The original rationale for it was as follows: profit is the reward for undertaking an activity, for investing one's capital, for running risks. Profit is also a measure of surplus of outputs over inputs. Surplus can be invested for further expansion, growth, and, thus, increased production of wealth. The main criticisms levelled at profit maximization have been the following: profits can be maximized by minimizing wages, expanding means of production, and increasing prices. Minimization of wages was socially objectionable, leading to the rich becoming richer and the poor becoming poorer, and economically self-defeating because it limited the demand for goods and services and, thus, the possibility for further expansion. Continued expansion of the means of production, it was argued, could only be achieved through conquests of colonial or foreign markets, thus engendering further conflicts and weakening of the system.

Wage minimization evoked several reactions and reforms: trade unions emerged, developed bargaining power, and forced substantial increases in wages in line with the increasing productivity and, sometimes, above it. Truly exploitative wages have been largely eliminated through minimum-wage legislation, passed in all free enterprise countries. As a result of the above, most people in free enterprise countries that have reached advanced stages of economic development have become richer and poverty has been largely eradicated. Economic inequalities have not been eliminated, but they have been reduced.

The second important design feature of the free enterprise system was private ownership of the means of production. The original moral justification for this was rooted in the so-called "natural right" to property, i.e. by application of effort to the commons man can transform it into private property. The more important rationale, though, has been the economic one. The reasoning was that it is the wealthy that can and do save and invest, leading to capital accumulation, expansion, growth, and subsequent prosperity for greater numbers. The accumulation of private property, therefore, is the ultimate reward of the efficient users of factors of production. The main criticism of this feature has been that, if unchecked, this process would lead to accumulation of wealth in fewer and fewer hands. To many, this seemed morally and politically unjust. It was also argued that, economically, it could be ineffective. While concentration of wealth favours investment, it limits the demand for consumption and, thereby, the need for further investment. The accumulation of wealth in fewer hands does not automatically lead to further economic expansion.

Demand, at least for consumption goods, it is argued, depends on the amount of purchasing power of the population and, therefore, is more related to equality rather than inequality in the distribution of wealth. Also, while economically it may be justifiable to allow the accumulation of wealth by the efficient users of it, the hereditary right to wealth is less justifiable, since there is no guarantee that the inheritors can make equally efficient use of it. Furthermore, while it is recognized that investments normally have to be made in big blocks rather than in very small slices, the alternative capital structures such as in Japan, where the bulk of investment capital is borrowed from banks, show that financial institutions can aggregate and package small savings into sufficiently large blocks for investment purposes. Concentrated holdings of capital in private hands are, therefore, not an indispensable precondition for capital accumulation.

The main reforms that have taken place to cope with the ill effects of wealth concentration have been progressive income and inheritance taxes, both of which help the process of diffusion of ownership rather than the predicted concentration of it. Huge family enterprises still exist on both sides of the Atlantic. However, they have become the exception rather than the rule. The dominant reality is widely spread ownership. This has brought about a fundamental transformation in the role of ownership in the free enterprise system. The diffusion, through shareholdings, has gradually diminished the ability of shareholders to have direct control over the means of production. The actual decisions as to what to produce, for what markets, through what combination of resources, and how to dispose of surpluses, are now in the hands of professional, nonowner managers of enterprises. The institutionalization of ownership through pension funds has taken this process even one step further. Direct shareholding at least allows a shareholder to dispose of his shares as a sign of dissatisfaction with results or evaluation of current policies and future prospects, and, thus, it is a measure of indirect influence over management. Entitlement to a pension gives no such rights. It is the trustees, the managers of the funds, who act on behalf of the real owners of such funds without, however, being controlled by them. Further limitations of the rights of owners, and now also of managers, have arisen in recent decades. Groups of people from the society, who feel affected by the functioning of an enterprise, form into constituencies and claim "stakeholder rights" to influence the conduct of an enterprise simply because they feel affected by its functioning.

The above explains what is meant by the statement "property without power and power without property". The authority, the right to dispose of resources, has changed over time in its very foundations. Initially, it was rooted in ownership. One could call that era one of "industrial aristocracy". It then shifted to competence, the technical ability of making economically effective use of resources. This, still predominant, state could be called the era of "professional meritocracy". The authority is again shifting, and will tend to stem from various constituencies. The "stakeholders" will have to approve, accept or at least acquiesce to managerial decisions. This next phase may perhaps be named the "stakeholder democracy".

The third, and perhaps the most crucial, feature of free enterprise is a free market. There are two different but converging kinds of justification for this design feature of the system. According to the first, free market means that there is competition for acquisition of resources and of factors of production. Since the most efficient users of resources generate the highest profits, they can offer the highest prices for them and thus acquire them most readily. This mechanism automatically ascertains the most productive use of available resources. The second justification has been provided by Adam Smith, who asserted that a free market acts like the invisible hand that guides individuals' pursuits of their economic self-interests towards the satisfaction of the interests of the greatest number.

There are, however, some intrinsic flaws, some observable malfunctioning in the free market mechanism; hence there are some strong criticisms against it. First, there is a propensity for cyclical variations in the level of economic activity. A demand for some product may go down. This can cause a chain reaction: reductions in demand are amplified by reduction of inventories, thus gradually intensifying the downturn. Experience has shown that if no intervention is made, an economy once started on a downturn can spiral into full depression. Secondly, there seem to be built-in, self-destructive forces in a free market. The market functions well, allocating factors of production to the more efficient, when there is true competition. This implies the existence of many small producers and buyers competing on the basis of price. The price reflects supply and demand conditions, since no one in particular is able to control the demand or supply. In practice such conditions rarely exist. Since profitability can be greatly improved by being able to control either supply or demand, and thus prices, it is in the short-term interest of the economic actors in the free market to develop the greatest possible influence over it. Whence the temptation of and drives for cartelization, monopolization, or, at least, for gaining a dominant share of any given market. Such situations can result in suboptimum use of resources. In this sense, entrepreneurs, who are the greatest believers in the virtues of a free market and its greatest protential benefactors, are at times its worst enemies.

As a result of these weaknesses of free markets and the criticisms levelled at them, some new instruments have developed, new policies have been adopted, and reforms have taken place. First, there has been the development of fiscal and monetary intervention techniques. A brief reminder of how they should function: when a downward cycle starts, purchasing power can be increased and fresh demand induced by increasing the volume of money in circulation and reducing its cost by lowering the interest rates on credits, mortgages, etc. The second measure, which in principle is equally effective but in reality is more difficult to apply, is to reduce taxes. The opposite measures can be applied when the demand for goods and services outstrips their supply, therefore causing inflation. To bring back the equilibrium between supply and demand, the volume of money in circulation can be reduced, its cost increased by raising the interest rates and by increasing taxes. Other instruments have been used to offset cyclical variations such as public-works types of investment, anticyclical budgeting, trying to balance cyclical variations in demand generated by the private sector with demand from public authorities. Recently, the fiscal and monetary instruments seem to have lost some of their effectiveness. The causes are more political than economic. It seems difficult for governments of the countervailing power type to maintain fiscal and monetary discipline; the fear of losing elections is too great.

Another reform was the promulgation of antitrust legislation, intended to protect competition from the corrosive effects of monopolization and cartelization. There are some difficulties with this instrument. When antitrust laws were originally introduced, say in the United States, the competitiveness of any enterprise was determined essentially on the domestic market. Now competitiveness is determined more on the international stage. Preventing mergers, acquisitions, or a dominant position on the domestic market can seriously inhibit the capacity of enterprises to do well in international competition, thus reducing the effectiveness of the whole economic system.

The next design feature of the free enterprise system was the limited role of government in economic affairs. Originally, government was expected simply to assure the proper functioning of the three determinants of the effectiveness of the system, i.e. maximization of profits, legitimacy and security of private ownership, and real freedom of markets. The justification for such a limited role was rooted in the belief that the pursuit of individual self-interests will assure satisfaction for the greatest number. This was the *laissez-faire* feature of capitalism, which by now has ceased to be a reality. Experience has shown that noninterference of government could mean excessive unemployment, great material and social inequalities, and predominance of individual over communal-public goals. A free market, when it functions well, means that resources are allocated to the highest bidder. It favours those who have something to offer. The young, vigorous, and competent can offer their energies and skills, command good salaries, assure their livelihood and even affluence. The sick, the less competent, or the old cease to be economic assets because they have nothing to offer on the market. There is no economic justification for them to be using any of the resources. If one follows this logic to its brutal extreme, such people should be scrapped, be sustained by relatives or friends, or, if they are wealthy, live off their inheritance. While the logic of the survival of the economically fittest is economi-

cally rigorous, it is socially and politically unacceptable in any contemporary society that acknowledges the right of each human being
to the satisfaction of at least their basic survival needs. We have seen,
therefore, a gradual expansion of the role of governments in correcting the distributive injustices of the marketplace through increasing
social legislation, old-age pensions, health insurance, unemployment
insurance, and general help to the needy. In this respect, the governments of free enterprise countries differ from distributive socialism
countries only in the degree of intervention within the free-market
mechanism.

The above analysis examined the forces that have moulded the
free enterprise system. By and large, it has performed well and has
enabled countries on both sides of the North Atlantic, at any rate, to
reach very advanced stages of economic development. Some fundamental questions can be raised though: Can this system be effective
for all countries, under all conditions of resource endowment, population growth, and density, and at all stages of economic development?
Under what conditions is this economic system most effective?

Some general propositions can be offered in answer to these questions. The free enterprise system seems highly effective when:

—the population is not growing dramatically, allowing gradual and
  voluntary capital accumulation, build-up of industry, and transfer
  of the population from agricultural to secondary sectors, enhancing
  their productivity and, through gradual infusion of technology,
  raising as well the productivity in agriculture;
—a country reaches the mass consumption stage of economic development during which satisfaction of individual consumption needs,
  particularly of consumer durables, convenience products, and
  luxury goods, is top priority, requiring a multitude of "free enterprises" with ability and motivation to respond to varying tastes
  and demands.

The system is not likely to be very effective when:

—population is growing very rapidly and new employment cannot be
  created rapidly enough through private initiatives;
—when resources are very scarce and need to be directed to obvious
  priority uses;

—when a country opts to go through a rapid industrialization period, particularly with a growing population and some resource constraints;

—when countries start reaching the postindustrial stages of economic development and priorities start shifting to such public consumption needs as clean environment, good education for all, health care, and interesting, not just remunerative, work for all.

The capitalist system was originally "designed" to excel in capital accumulation and efficient production of wealth. Gradually, its abuses and malfunctioning have been corrected and social and political considerations incorporated into its functioning. There are now other forces at work that will modify the system again and in some ways make it converge with other systems whose analysis follows.

CONCERTED FREE ENTERPRISE

The main characteristics of this system are very similar to those of "free enterprise". Profitability is the key precondition of long-term survival of enterprises and, thus, an important criterion by which their performance is judged. Private ownership of means of production is predominant. There is broad diffusion of ownership through shareholding. The market is relatively free with a number of suppliers and buyers, and prices are determined as a function of supply, demand, and costs of production.

The system differs from the "purer" form of free enterprise by the degree of harmonization of economic objectives within the business community, the degree of consultation between business, government, and, in some cases, labour leaders, hence the capacity to evolve national economic objectives and priorities without resorting to imperative planning or administrative allocation of resources. Three variants of the system are analysed here—the French, West German, and Japanese, listed in ascending order of efficacy of the system as manifested by the overall economic performance of the countries concerned.

The expression "concerted" as applied to an economic system is of French inspiration and it is in *France* that its historical roots are probably the deepest. They can be traced back to the seventeenth century of Louis XIV and his minister of finance, J. B. Colbert, who established some state companies and a strong governmental directing hand over the economic life of the country. The modern reincarnation of Colbertism surfaced after the Second World War in the form of indicative planning and some nationalized enterprises. A General Planning Commissariat was established in 1946 as the main instrument for guiding the French economy while leaving the bulk of ownership in private hands and letting the market forces do the bulk of allocation and distribution of resources.*

There was a succession of three- to five-year plans that have taken France through reconstruction, growth, and some restructuring of the economy. The process of planning has been fairly complex. First, an overall rate of economic development was set. Specific plans were then elaborated in various commissions in which representatives from the respective sectors of economic activities compared their plans, investment proposals, etc. The output of the commissions would be compared in order to work out imbalances, likely over- or under-capacities. An overall scheme with specific sectoral plans would emerge. Such plans did not have the power of law. To ensure their implementation, government relied heavily on capital allocation through nationalized banks and credit policies. This made it possible to favour the expansion of "desired" activities and impede undesired ones.

There are other reasons why a fair amount of harmonization of economic activity can take place in France and why the government can exercise so much influence on the economic life of the country. The most important one is probably the existence of an élite civil service, a professional administration *mandarinat*. These are graduates of high-quality élitist *grandes écoles* and the National School of Administration where they develop the capacity for hard and competent work, some shared perceptions about their nation's destiny, and dedication to it. This network maintains the traditional centralizing trends and ascertains the priority of national over particular objectives. There is also a strongly organized *patronat* that can voice the

*Kindelberger, C. P., *French Planning in Comparative Economic Systems*, Richard D. Irwin, Homewood, Ill., 1969.

opinions of business and industrial leaders after consultations in sectoral committees.

The expansion of economic activity, its greater complexity, greater opening to international trade, made indicative planning more difficult and somewhat less effective. In recent years, there has been a greater reliance on market forces, with "concertation" accomplished by making all the signals point in the same direction. In the case of the energy problem, for instance, this has been done by sharing information about it, pushing the petrol prices up, heavy publicity on energy saving, thus "consciousness raising", and of course credits to alternate energy sources.

The effectiveness of the above system is constrained by sharp ideological and political party divisions and the fact that much of organized labour is hostile to the system and kept outside of the power structure.

The Federal Republic of Germany seems resolutely committed to the free enterprise system yet is able at the same time to ascertain a high degree of harmonization and direction of its economy without resorting to central planning or administrative compulsion. A number of factors and institutional arrangements contribute to this.

Firstly, there is the tradition, since Bismarck, of government assuming a supportive role to business through tariff protection or direct participation via state companies.

Secondly, there is some predisposition of the population to societal discipline and subordination to higher purposes. Even more important are the very extensive consultative processes, the legislation emerging therefrom, and the role of the banks in influencing the directions of industrial and business activities.

Both employers and employees are strongly organized under powerful umbrella federations. There is little special-interest lobbying of the American type. Individual companies do not go to the government or the parliamentarians. They first meet in their associations and speak to the government through their federations.

The bureaucrats of the executive branch carry out intensive consultations with various interest groups as a basis for policy formulation and legislative proposals. It is the executive branch that elaborates the legislative proposals by guiding the economic life of the country.

The parliamentarians debate and pass laws, but they have no staffs, hence do not prepare laws.

Banks own shares in a broad spectrum of companies, supply them with credits, and can influence heavily their key decisions. This contributes further to some harmonization of business activities.

It is the combination of a government generally sympathetic to business with less separation between legislative and executive branches, with strongly organized employers and labour, powerful banks, and extensive consultation between these various elements of the power structure that enables Germany to make good economic music without having to sing in unison.

If such a prize were to exist, *Japan* would get the first prize for the orchestration of economic activity while maintaining a basically free enterprise system. The remarkable economic performance of Japan over the last few decades is an eloquent manifestation of the efficacy of the system. From a very secondary position it now almost equals the United States in GNP per capita and it surpasses it by a factor of ten in GNP per square kilometre of land.*

There are a number of factors that contribute to rendering the economy so effective:

—First and foremost, the cultural values make it natural and almost imperative for the Japanese to subordinate individual or small-group interest to "higher purposes" like national economic performance.

—Secondly, the intrinsic nature of the Japanese decision-making process contains a strong *penchant* for conflict avoidance and discussions of issues and problems with all involved. Development of consensus is a slow, tedious process, but one that ascertains subsequent adhesion to decisions.

—Thirdly, there are the institutional arrangements, i.e. organization of government, industry, and labour.

—Fourthly, there exists a competent and dedicated administrative élite.†

*Okita, S., Japan, China, and the United States: relations and prospects, *Foreign Affairs*, Summer 1979, **57** (5).

†Vogel, F. E., Guided free enterprise in Japan, *Harvard Business Review*, May–June 1978, **56** (3).

The first two elements have already been discussed earlier in the book. The last two merit a little elaboration.

The government perceives its key role to be the facilitation rather than the regulation of business activity. It relies more on "administrative guidelines", influence over credit facilities, and instruments like plant construction licences than regulations or laws to make companies adhere to set objectives. Legislators who do not get "personal constituency" support and have no personal staffs must rely on the executive branch for the preparation of laws. The Ministry of International Trade and Industry (MITI) makes studies, forecasts, sets goals and objectives, and communicates them all broadly. The Ministry of Finance (MOF) controls the Bank of Japan, which lends money to big banks, which supply the bulk of capital to companies. Since it also controls the tax system, the MOF can heavily influence the adherence to guidelines supplied by MITI.

Both bodies, but particularly MITI, involve industry in an extensive consultative process. Big industry plays a dominant role and is organized into three traditional "conglomerates" (*zaibatsus*) and more recent groups centred around three big banks. There is a great deal of consultation and policy harmonization within such groups. Then there are trade associations organized along sectoral lines, where further consultations take place, and, finally, the powerful umbrella organization of all major firms, the Keidanren, which provides the forum for discussion of all key economic issues, speaks for business interests, and whose professional staffs prepare a lot of studies used by various ministries as policy inputs. Since labour is organized mainly in company unions, and given the life employment practice in the big firms, it sees its interest as largely coinciding with those of their companies. Labour leaders carry on consultations among themselves also and are consulted by some government bodies.

There are conflicts of interests, some companies get hurt while others, whose activities are in line with governmental objectives, get favoured, but there is a general recognition that things are done for the overall interest of the country.

In addition to the general predisposition to conflict avoidance, consultation, and cooperation, it is an élite core of bureaucrats (recruited mainly from the prestigious faculty of law from the equally prestigious university of Tokyo) that makes the system function so effectively. Due to a tough selection process, the bureaucrats in question are intelligent, competent, hard working, and unquestionably dedicated. They are not necessarily loved, sometimes even disliked for their arrogance, but rarely questioned on their competence or commitment to the service of the nation. They have moral authority, shored up by carrots and sticks, which enhances their persuasiveness.

There are some common features in the various forms of the "concerted free enterprise" described above. Firstly, the governments see as one of their main roles the facilitation rather than just the regulation or control of economic activity. The legislative and executive branches of such governments are not sharply separated and certainly not countering each other, so that legislation and administration are better harmonized.

Secondly, the various economic interest groups are broadly based, well organized, all playing according to the rules of the game and conscious of broad national interests. Thirdly, there are consultative processes that are well designed and rigorously adhered to. Finally, there are competent, dedicated, and rather permanent administrative élites.

Given the above preconditions, the greater the general acceptance of the "rightness" of the system and predisposition toward co-operative relations between government, business, and labour, the more effectively the system seems to function.

COMMAND-STATE ENTERPRISE

This label identifies the source of economic authority, initiative, and key decisions, as well as state ownership and control of the means of production. The most representative of this type of economic system is that found in the Soviet Union. It has been inspired by egalitarian-collectivist values, founded on Marxist ideology, born out of analysis of and as a reaction to capitalism. The following have been the main underlying postulates: economic relations determine all others. The ultimate purpose of a societal order, hence of its economic system, should be full economic equality. Capitalism is based on economic inequalities and the exploitation of workers through the appropriation by owners of the surplus value generated by workers. While the capitalist system has mobilized and unleashed great productive forces, it is doomed to collapse because of its internal contradictions and conflicts between classes. Its collapse should be precipitated through proletarian revolutions.

The 1917 October Revolution was the first such event. Many analysts argue that the October Revolution took place in the wrong country since Czarist Russia had not reached a sufficently advanced stage of capitalist development. Western European countries were theoretically more ripe for revolutions because of their advanced degrees of industrialization, development of the proletariat class, and political consciousness. Since, however, much social-economic progress was being achieved in Western Europe through peaceful democratic-parliamentary means, there was not enough predisposition toward revolution among the working classes in that part of the world. In the Czarist Russian Empire, the Revolution did succeed for a variety of reasons. The Czarist regime was left without much support among the population. Some of the aristocracy felt that the regime was becoming too liberal, too progressive. The intelligentsia felt that it was not progressive enough. Peasants were still hungry for land, workers were being exploited, and the non-Russian nationalities were oppressed. The army was seriously demoralized by the military setbacks of the First World War. On the other side were Lenin's mobilizing slogans such as "land to peasants, freedom to non-Russian nationalities, power to the proletariat", and a small but disciplined and dedicated group of revolutionaries. What had helped tip the balance was the fact that the decadent regime, with Western help, seemed at times more anxious to crush national liberation movements than the communist revolution.

The Soviet economy went through a series of stages that moulded it to its present shape. First, there was the "war communism" phase from 1918 to 1922. It was characterized by the takeover of industrial, banking, and commercial enterprises, elimination of owners, and the institution of workers' councils. Because of lack of technical and managerial competence of the new people in charge, the suppression of normal commercial relations, and the elimination of monetary incentives, the economic performance during that period was very poor. In order to put the economy back on its feet, the "New Economic Policy" was introduced. Private ownership of small-scale undertakings was restituted and commercial relations reestablished. Within a few years the economy was reconstructed and its output restored to its prewar level.

In 1929, the new economic policy was abolished and a phase of rapid, forced-draft industrialization was started with the first five-year plan. There were several converging reasons for the adoption of this new direction. The free enterprise nature of the new economic policy was an ideological concession and was thought to be embarking the Soviet Union on a course contrary to its political objectives. The pace of industrialization and modernization was judged inadequate. It was felt necessary to protect the Soviet Union from the hostile surrounding world and to back up subsequent proletariat revolutions abroad; therefore, a strong army was needed and this, in turn, required a strong industrial base.

The new policy had a number of components. First, there was the forcible collectivization of agriculture. Its purposes were to abolish private property in agriculture, facilitate larger-scale cultivation and mechanization, release some labour from agriculture to industry, establish full control over production and supply of food to the growing urban–industrial population, and to skim the surpluses from agriculture for financing of industrial investment. The second component of the policy was the priority given to the development of an energy base, metallurgical and machine-building industries, and physical infrastructure. The third element was the decision to maintain high rates of investment by curbing current consumption. All of the above was implemented through central planning, administrative allocation of resources, and the integration of all economic units through the state apparatus. But for the disruptions of the Second World War this phase of economic development lasted until the early 1960s. By that time the basic economic objectives were achieved, the take-off was accomplished, and an extensive industrial base was created. As the economy began to mature, the priorities changed and some reforms of the economic system were hesitantly undertaken.

There were significant social and political costs associated with the above accomplishments, such as massive starvation during collectivi-

TABLE 6. *Evolution of command-state enterprise system*

Key features	Ensuing problems and criticisms	Reactions and reforms
1. *Maximization of outputs* Through quantitative targets for fast industrialization; subsequent affluence	Distortions due to single success indicators; wastages; useless goods	Multiplication of success indicators; introduction of value-added indicators; resuscitation of profitability
2. *State ownership* To eliminate inequalities of wealth; assure rational use of means of production	Insufficient rewards for performance; inefficient enterprises survive; suboptimum use of resources	Individual performance incentives; share of surpluses kept by enterprises; private plots in agriculture (private ownership of most land in Poland)
3. *Administered market* Resources to priority sectors; full utilization of facilities; resources; stability; self-sufficiency	Prices not reflecting costs; misuse of capital; poor quality of consumer goods; inadequate international specialization/competitiveness	Reform of some prices to reflect costs; interest on capital; free market prices for some goods; more international trade
4. *Determinant role of government* Clear objectives; priorities; preference to public over private needs	Multiplication of priorities; bottlenecks; growing complexity of central planning; bureaucratization	Some decentralization; some commercial relations between enterprises
5. *Original rationale and objectives* Mainly political; to change property relations and create material base for introduction of communism	Distortions due to rejection of "economic laws" such as the cost of scarcity	Gradually "natural economic laws" are recognized and partly integrated into the system

zation, subsequent chronic undersupply of consumer goods, and, of course, the Stalinist terror. No in-depth analysis of such costs is made here since the purpose is to focus on the mechanisms and functioning of various economic systems, to enhance the understanding of how the various sets of values, types of political governance, and economic systems match or mismatch, and how their functioning can be improved.

With this brief historical background, the key design features of the command-state enterprise economic model, some of its intrinsic weaknesses, and the ensuing reforms will now be examined and an attempt made to distil the direction of its evolution. The analysis is summarized in Table 6.

The first feature of the command-state enterprise system is its focus on the maximization of outputs. Since communism was seen as the ultimate objective, the introduction of its fundamental rule "to each according to his needs" required first the creation of a base for material affluence. The architects of the system thought that the best way to create it was by giving to each economic unit a clear quantitative output target. Maximization of profits was ideologically objectionable, since it was seen as an instrument for the exploitation of workers. Therefore, instead of judging the performance of enterprises and their management by the amount of profits generated, they were to be judged using the degree of fulfilment or overfulfilment of the quantitative output targets as "success indicators".

This method invites distortions. There are various ways of maximizing output by using excessive amounts of capital, labour, machinery, or raw materials. The distortions can be particularly great when a product does not have a single dominant characteristic or a quality standard. One can produce the planned number of water taps, for instance, by using substandard materials and poor workmanship, but such taps are not likely to function well, will require frequent repairs, or become unusable. The requisite tonnage of roofing sheet can be more readily produced by using up more rolled stock, thus wastage of raw material, by doing a poor job of tin-plating or by using more expensive machinery and applying more manpower. There is another difficulty with quantitative targets: since output quotas are fixed by planning organs after getting the production capacity estimates from the enterprises, the natural tendency for the enterprise is to underestimate their capacities in order to get easy-to-accomplish quantitative targets. This leads to discussions and even "bargaining" between the different organs concerned and setting of targets that can be either below or above the real. capacity, with a consequent suboptimum use of facilities and resources.

This intrinsic flaw of the system evoked a lot of criticisms and attempts at corrective actions. At first, this was done by increasing the number of success indicators. Let us follow up the example of roofing sheet. An enterprise, instead of getting a single target such as square metres of roofing sheet, would get a number of objectives and norms such as output specified in tons and square metres of various gauges, per cent of recovery of stock, man-hours per unit output, etc. Multiplication of success indicators, however, complicates managerial decision-making without providing enough rational criteria for resource allocations, because of yet another fundamental difficulty of this type of economic system. The enterprises are not responsible for selling, for disposing of, their output. There is, thus, no built-in incentive for them to assure product quality and utility. It appears extremely difficult to come up with success indicators other than profitability that measure the difference of useful outputs over inputs of an enterprise. Some indicators of value-added were introduced in various Eastern European countries but, more important, profitability was partly resuscitated and reintroduced. Part of the planning process now is for many enterprises to have, in addition to some quantitative success indicators, a profit target and be judged on its achievement.

State ownership of the means of production is the second key feature of this type of economic system. There is a dual rationale behind this. Private ownership can allow exploitation and can enhance economic inequalities, class differences, and conflicts. In Marxist ideology, private ownership is a basic social ill. Also, the takeover by the state of all means of production was expected to lead to a more rational use of all resources, increase outputs, and thus help prepare the material base for the introduction of communism. This particular feature also has inherent weaknesses. Many people exhibit acquisitive instincts; if there is no opportunity for them to retain and multiply the fruits of their effort, their efforts tend to diminish. This has been observed particularly in the agricultural sector. Labour in agriculture appears to be partly a labour of love. The proprietary interest in land seems to increase the incentive to work. Also, private ownership in combination with a free market imposes the discipline of economic efficiency by the ultimate threat of bankruptcy. This automatically engenders the incentive to work and assures the economic use of resources. When all the enterprises are owned by the state, which also has noneconomic objectives such as full employment, the inefficient enterprises are allowed to continue to operate, resulting in less than optimum use of resources.

Measures to offset some of these difficulties have been taken at least for the period of transition to communism. Thus individual monetary incentives based on performance have been reintroduced. Enterprises are allowed to keep and dispose of part of the surpluses that they generate. This provides the enterprises, and particularly their management, with an incentive to function efficiently, since managers' earnings also depend on this. In the agricultural sector, private plots are allowed on which the collective farm workers can cultivate produce for their own consumption and for sale on relatively free markets in order to supplement their inadequate earnings from the collective farms. Some Eastern European countries, notably Poland, have restituted most of the land to private ownership.

The third design feature of command-state enterprise is the administered market. It was felt that by centrally deciding on and controlling who is to produce what, with what inputs, and to whom to transfer at which prices, it should be possible for the state to direct the resources to priority growth sectors, to ascertain full use of all production facilities and resources, and, thereby, to assure economic stability, full employment, and a high degree of economic self-sufficiency. For the Soviet Union, autarky seemed economically possible because of its size and broad range of natural resource endowments. It was politically desirable because of the intention to protect and expand the communist revolution. This feature of the system also has some inherent problems. When prices are set administratively according to other than purely economic criteria, they cease to reflect the true cost of inputs. The resulting arbitrary prices cause some wastages and misuse of scarce resources. It was decided, for instance, that for ideological reasons there would be no cost of capital, no interest rates applied. This has led, in a number of sectors of activity, to unduly capital-intensive modes of production.

A further difficulty arises as the economy starts diversifying and the number of products multiplies. The number of prices to be fixed centrally increases, causing bureaucratic expansion and inefficiencies. Yet another difficulty is the impact of such price setting on the quality of consumer goods. It is easy to set administratively a price for a quantity, but it is very much more difficult to set it according to some quality criterion. Finally, arbitrary pricing warps the understanding of comparative advantages of the economy, rendering more difficult foreign-trade decisions.

Various measures and reforms have been attempted to cope with these difficulties. Periodic price reviews have taken place in order to bring pricing closer to efficiency pricing. Interest on capital has been reintroduced in recognition of the fact that a zero interest rate implies an infinite supply of capital, and, therefore, an abusive use of it. Since, however, this interest was set arbitrarily and across the board, it is not sufficiently reflective of the demand for capital or alternate uses of it. In order to reduce the burden of central price fixing, goods have been put into several different categories. Prices for strategic goods are fixed centrally; for intermediary goods, price ranges are also fixed centrally; and for goods of strictly local nature and importance, prices are established according to the law of supply and demand.

Foreign-trade decisions have been based mainly on input/output analysis. When an economic plan is being made, an analysis is carried out to show what inputs are likely to be short and what surpluses are likely to arise or can be generated. The first are imported and the second are destined for export. World prices, rather than domestic ones, are used for transaction purposes. Some indices have developed to give an approximate assessment of comparative advantage. Foreign trade has expanded partly to import avant-garde technology with which to offset yet another difficulty—the inadequate rate of conversion of theoretical scientific knowledge into new products or more efficient processes.

The next characteristic feature of this economic system is the determinant role of government in all economic matters. The rationale behind it was to be able to set, through its planning organs, clear objectives and priorities, to give preference to public over private needs, and to allocate all resources accordingly.

Total control by the government of economic life is easier at early, primitive stages of economic development when there are few priorities. With diversification of the economy there is a multiplication of priorities and an increasing complexity of planning, administration, and control. The complexity seems to increase as an exponential rather than a linear function of the growth in size and diversity of the economy. This generates an information overload and communication difficulties, with resulting bottlenecks, temporary crises, and continued expansion of bureaucracy. At various times during the last few decades, attempts at some reforms have been made to offset these difficulties. There was the creation of economic regions, their subsequent regrouping, the decentralization of some economic decision-making, and the establishment of commercial relations between production and distribution enterprises.

The key considerations in the design of the above economic system were essentially political, i.e. to change property relations and to create the material base for the introduction of communism. This rationale dictated the four main design features, i.e. maximization of outputs, state ownership, an administered market, and the central role of government. Each one of these features, separately and through interaction with each other, have led to some distortions. In attempts to offset them, more orthodox economic criteria have been introduced into the decision-making process. The main ones are profitability as the best and simplest criterion by which to measure the performance of an enterprise, and pricing more reflective of costs to assure better use of scarce resources. Partial integration of these and other "natural economic laws" into the economy has been the essential direction of the evolution of the system. Some countries that fashioned their economic systems according to the Soviet model, such as Hungary, have reformed their economies even more substantially.

It is evident from the above that while a command-state enterprise remains very different from free enterprise as far as the nature of ownership of the means of production is concerned, it tends to approach it in the use of monetary incentives, the profitability criteria, and some aspects of the free market as an allocator of resources. This justifies the observation that there is some convergence between the two, heretofore ideologically opposed, systems.

While the above analysis points out many difficulties that have arisen as well as the modifications that have been made to the original design of the command-state enterprise economic system, it is an undisputable fact that the Soviet Union did emerge rapidly as one of the biggest industrial powers in the world. The economic system adopted by it has clearly been instrumental in its rapid industrialization. Should one conclude, therefore, that this type of system is the most effective and has a model value for many societies with different resource endowments and at different stages of development? Hardly. As with any economic system, this one is highly effective under certain conditions and quite ineffective under others. It produces some distinctive benefits, but also imposes some high costs.

Among the advantages of the system are the possibility to:

—establish firm priorities and allocate resources to them: one can thus focus sequentially, for instance, on building up an energy base, heavy industry, and a physical infrastructure, following the pattern established by other countries;
—restrain consumption and increase rates of investment;
—favour public consumption, such as education or health care, over private consumption, such as cars;
—assure full employment.

There are some disadvantages, such as:

—the need for imposition of discipline and regimentation;
—the enforced postponement of satisfaction of personal consumption needs;
—the generally low quality of consumer goods;
—the difficulty of being in the avant-garde of commercially useful technological innovations, since it is easier to replicate through planning the existing things than to facilitate the invention of new ones;
—the lack of competitiveness on international markets, except in resource-based exports or in relatively simple products.

It seems legitimate to suggest that the command-state enterprise economic system can be effective under the following conditions:

—in a country with a broad range of resource endowments, thus potential economic autarky;

—in countries with excessive population, where employment of people even in low-productivity pursuits is better than massive unemployment;

—under emergency situations where rationing and allocation of resources is the only way to meet basic requirements;

—for going rapidly through the early stages of industrialization, especially the economic take-off stage.

As a country reaches a more advanced state of industrial development and could physically move into the mass consumption stage, the command type of economic system becomes unwieldy and unresponsive—more of a constraint than a facilitator. Only by having multiple points at which economic decisions can be made and initiatives undertaken can a system respond to the diversity of demands from the population. On the other hand, one can postulate that once the countries move past the mass consumption stage, and communal public consumption needs assume greater importance, a larger role for government in economic life may be indispensable; hence, some features of the command type of economy may be more effective than the pure free enterprise system in which a free market is the sole allocator.

DISTRIBUTIVE SOCIALISM

This economic system is an interesting combination of socialist objectives and, mainly, free enterprise system. It exists in various versions in Scandinavian countries, but the example of Sweden may be the most suitable for this particular analysis. The underlying idea is the separation of the two economic functions: the creation of wealth and its distribution. The first is left in the hands of the private, free enterprise sector. The second is accomplished by heavy intervention of the government to offset and correct the perceived distributive injustices of the otherwise free market. The main contours, with some of the problems and consequences, are summarized in Table 7.

TABLE 7. *Evolution of distributive socialism*

Key features	Ensuing problems and criticisms	Reactions and reforms
1. *Profit maximization* Good incentive for effort; discipline on firms in use of resources	High taxes and social security reduce individual motivation when work not a condition of survival	Increasing intrinsic motivation through participation; quality of work conditions; social rewards of work
2. *Private ownership* Arbitrary dispossession seen as unjust and economically ineffective	Some private groups; banks still have a dominant role in the economy	High taxes to reduce accumulation; proposed gradual institutionalization of ownership by unions
3. *Free market* Best allocator of resources, particularly of individual consumption goods	Propensity for cyclical variations; regional inequalities; dying of some industrial sectors	Tax incentives for anti-cyclical and regional equalization investments; help for restructuring
4. *Role of government* To facilitate production of wealth in socially just ways and to assure equitable distribution	Big bureaucracy, reducing initiative; burdensome "provident state", inducing boredom	Concerns about loss of international competitiveness; attempts to slow down growth of bureaucracy
5. *Original rationale and objectives* Free enterprise excels in production of wealth; role of socialist government is to ascertain distributive justice	Dilemma between efficiency, thus incentives, small overheads, and equality in incomes; opportunities; social security	Smallness of countries concerned; needs for imports/exports; thus international competitiveness set outer limits on distributive justice

Let us now examine in somewhat greater detail the main design features of this system. Profit maximization is accepted as the motivator of and the key criterion for judging the performance of enterprises. Profits are seen as a measure of surplus of outputs over inputs, thus the evidence of the economic use of resources. The abusive ways of maximizing profits through minimization of wages are not feared, given the power of the unions and, backing them, the socialist government, which was in power for over forty years. This is reflected in legislation that prevents any form of exploitation or misuse of power vested in the enterprises.

The concerns that have been expressed and the problems that have emerged relating to profit maximization have centred on the difficulty of sustaining an adequate profitability to support investment and innovation for continued viability. The profitable operation of enterprise requires, among other things, a significant amount of motivation of the people within them. Given highly progressive taxation on one side and a high degree of social security on the other, work is financially less rewarding and has ceased to be a dire economic necessity, thereby impairing the motivation to work. To offset these negative effects, many measures have been undertaken both at the level of individual firms and at the national macro-level through legislation. The main thrust of the former has been to compensate for the reduced extrinsic motivation to work (high pay for good work) by increasing the intrinsic motivation to work. This is being done through increasing the opportunity for workers to influence decisions affecting their work, upgrading the quality of work and its intrinsic challenge, improving the physical conditions of work, enhancing social rewards of work through greater autonomy of work teams, reducing hierarchial differences—in short, enhancing the dignity of man at work. After some voluntary experimentation, worker participation in management at the board level has been legislatively imposed. The purpose is to give a greater "stake" to those most affected by the life of the enterprises, to increase their commitment and responsibility, and, thus, to enhance their economic effectiveness.

Private ownership is antithetical to the socialist ideology that favours communal, collective, or state ownership. It has been accepted, though, as the main form of ownership and is tolerated for several reasons. First, private ownership was the inherited state of affairs when the socialists came to power in Sweden. Sudden, massive nationalization would not have been possible to bring about in a democratic fashion and would have had economically disruptive effects. Secondly, arbitrary and sudden dispossession of people did not appear politically just. The most important considerations were probably of the economic kind. The experience of other countries seemed to show that free enterprise, of which private property was an important component, seemed to be an efficient system for production of wealth. Nationalizations, where they took place, did not automatically increase the economic efficiency of the countries concerned, and often the result was quite the opposite. It was thought, therefore, that government may not have the comparative advantage in direct management of production and distribution enterprises. As a result, and despite four decades of socialist government in Sweden, the overwhelming proportion of the means of production has remained in private hands. Only a small part is in the form of cooperative ownership, with some five per cent owned directly by the state.

The criticisms that have been levelled at this particular feature of the system have focused on the fact that some families, small private groups, and banks continue to play a dominant role in the economy. In order to reduce the accumulation and concentration of wealth and to promote its diffusion, highly progressive taxation has been instituted. Furthermore, the intention for the future was to bring about a gradual shift in ownership to unions through acquisition of company shares, to be financed out of company profits. Had the policy been applied, unions would have acquired controlling positions within a couple of decades. Ownership would not have shifted to the workers themselves, however. It would have taken a more collective, institutionalized form. The recent change in the government has shelved this particular set of proposals.

The next important component of this economic system is freedom of markets. It was felt that a free market was an efficient allocator of resources for productive purposes and distributor of individual consumption goods. Prices that reflect supply and demand conditions allocate factors of production more efficiently than administered prices would. Another consideration was, of course, the fact that

Sweden is highly dependent on foreign trade; hence, its domestic prices have to reflect the external ones. As in other countries, a free market has an intrinsic propensity to cyclical variations and potential regional inequalities caused, in turn, by climatic conditions, natural resource distribution, and topography. To cope with such fluctuations, various instruments were developed. One of them allowed firms to deposit in special accounts 50 per cent of their profits before taxes. They could withdraw the funds without paying taxes if they invested them in periods and places agreed upon by the government. This is an interesting form of tax incentive for anticyclical and regional equalization investments.

The primary thrust of governmental activity has been focused on offsetting the distributive injustices of the free market through highly progressive taxation, highly advanced social legislation, and welfare measures, including free education, health care, generous unemployment insurance, and old-age pensions. The government also saw among its roles the maintenance of the administrative, legal, and some of the physical infrastructure in order to facilitate the functioning of the private sector. In addition to assuring both the efficient production of wealth and distributive justice, the government also tried to make sure that the production of wealth would take place in "socially just" ways with good working conditions, reduced hazards, and with an equilibrium of forces between management and labour.

Concerns and criticisms have focused mainly on the very high and progressive taxes, the heavy bureaucracy, and the burdensome, omnipresent, and omnipotent "provident" state. The consequences that were seen to flow from the provident state were: increasing overhead costs, loss of international competitiveness, the resulting need for rapid industrial restructuring, and the consequent need for the government to step in and take over ailing industries.

The original rationale and purpose of distributive socialism were quite clear: separation of production of wealth and its distribution, with the first left in the private sector, thought to excel in it, and the second one heavily moderated by the government. This poses the dilemma and sharpens the question of whether there is an incompatibility between economic efficiency and economic equality. The former seems to require incentives and motives, and therefore differentiation in rewards, while the second one calls for reduction of such a differentiation in order to ascertain the equality of incomes, opportunities, influence, and social position. The thrust for attaining an even greater equality, for bringing about a major change in the nature of property ownership, is likely to be moderated by the necessity for a country like Sweden to maintain its export capacity and, thus, its international competitiveness based on domestic economic efficiency. This is what sets the outer limits on the ultimate social and political objective of this system—the achievement of full distributive justice.

While the objective was a substantial transformation of the society, the process opted for was evolutionary rather than revolutionary. Gradual but early improvement in the economic welfare of the population was preferred to sacrifices by the present generation against promises of a bright future. Increasing equality was backed by popular will. Full legality and political freedoms have been maintained rather than imposing political discipline and subordination upon the masses in order to prepare a just and desirable future order.

As pointed out, distributive socialism has generated some sharp criticisms, both within the countries concerned and from outside. Governmental care from cradle to grave is contrary to individualistic ideas of initiative, self-help, and personal responsibility for one's destiny. Extreme social security is seen by many as being demobilizing and reducing the motivation to work—as evidenced in Sweden, for instance, by high degrees of absenteeism and labour turnover. Another fear concerns the possible general weakening of the moral fibre. Other criticisms centre on the fact that while legality and constitutional freedoms are guaranteed, the heavy hand of government imposes great administrative constraints and limitations, thereby, in fact, reducing true freedoms. Yet another reservation has been that distributive socialism, in its advanced stage, induces values, habits, and behaviour that are suitable only for a postindustrial, highly affluent society. Sweden, as a country, may be close to that state but, because of its economic interdependence with other countries that have not yet reached that state, it may have a tough time maintaining its economic viability on the world's economic chessboard.

The performance of this system has been generally positive for some four decades. The rate of technological progress has been high.

There has been significant upgrading and reorientation of industrial activity towards higher productivity and higher value-added types of operations. The resulting rates of economic growth have been high and accompanied by a significant reduction of economic inequalities. This calls for some qualification: while distributive socialism may have contributed significantly to the above, there have been other causes of progress, such as some natural resource endowments, high political maturity of the population with its predisposition to cooperation, the resulting industrial peace, the absence of sharp social conflicts, and, hence, the possibility of channelling energies into rather productive uses. The main question that has been hanging over the system during the last few years is the following: the expectation for continued progress towards social and economic equality and improved welfare develops its own momentum. Will there be a political compulsion to maintain such progress even when it cannot be economically sustained because of a slowdown in economic growth and inadequate increases of productivity? The utility of distributive socialism as a model to other societies depends on its ability to cope with the above dilemma.

MARKET SOCIALISM

The particular economic system has evolved in Yugoslavia. The summary analysis of the "building blocks" used in its construction, the criticisms levelled at it, and the direction of its evolution are summarized in Table 8.

The core ideas underlying the design of this system have been the following: it is principally workers who produce value and surpluses. Therefore they should control the means of production and have the ultimate say about the disposal of the surpluses that they create. This cannot be achieved by government managing the whole economy on behalf of the workers, even though the government is rooted in the party of the proletariat. Those within any given enterprise should be able to influence directly the decisions as to what work needs to be done, how it is to be carried out, who their bosses should be, and what the financial rewards should be.

TABLE 8. *Evolution of market socialism*

Key features	Ensuing problems and criticisms	Reactions and reforms
1. *Viability of enterprises* Both profitability and maximum outputs	Difficulties of marriage of socialist objectives and capitalist efficiency criteria	Legal constraints on enterprise autonomy; ideological admonitions
2. *Ownership* By workers' collectives. labour creates value thus property, it should control it	Lack of competence to manage; rubber stamping; short-term interests prevail over long-term investments; cumbersome in agriculture and small-service enterprises	Education of workers; professionalization of management; rules for distribution of surpluses; much land and small-service enterprises back to private hands
3. *"Concerted" free market* Good allocator of resources	Monopoly of some enterprises; inefficient can survive; unemployment; technological lags	Encouraging domestic competition; exposure to foreign competition; "exporting" labour to free enterprise countries; joint ventures with foreign companies
4. *Government "orchestrates"* Sets objectives; coordinates; regulates; assures political power	No master plan; suboptimum investments; regionalism	Directing investments through credit policy; more political controls over economic activity
5. *Original objectives* Workers' autonomy and self-management	Problems of reconciling national interests and autonomy of workers' collectives	Oscillation between central control and enterprise autonomy. between ideology and economic rigour

The Yugoslav system has thus been conceived as a direct rather than a representative economic democracy. In the latter type, power is exercised in the name of the workers, presumably for their good, but without them having any direct say about it. The case of Yugoslavia constitutes, therefore, a real social innovation. Many difficulties have emerged in practice, but the experimentation continues. There is apparently a genuine will to come up with a new societal model rather than just to use a set of slogans to mobilize popular support for a new political regime. This model has stimulated some thinking and experimentation with worker participation in free enterprise countries and in distributive socialism countries, though in substantially different forms.

The first of the features of market socialism is viability as the main motivation and criterion by which performance of enterprises is judged. One of the workers' primary motives should be to assure the viability of their enterprise. It must generate some surpluses (profits) for future investments, for technological innovations, and for expansion. National good demands that outputs also be maximized. Some of the difficulties that arise from the above are the following: it is in the spirit of socialism to serve communal needs and to prepare the basis for future material affluence. Each enterprise should act according to what the national good demands, as reflected in governmental priorities, plans, and directives. The survival of an enterprise demands, however, that attention be paid to efficiency and profitability—in other words, that it be managed according to orthodox capitalist criteria. The difficulty of crossbreeding socialist objectives with capitalist instruments has resulted in the imposition of legal constraints on the autonomy of the enterprise and in the application of political and ideological pressures on enterprises through party and government channels.

The ownership of most of the means of production is collective in nature. Workers within an enterprise do not have individual property rights in it. They can exercise their group-communal right as long as they are working within the enterprise; this they can do directly and through elected representatives. The justification for this form of ownership has been essentially Marxist. According to Marx, since labour creates all wealth, it should control the means to the production of wealth. As stated above, in Yugoslavia workers control directly rather than through the party or the government acting on their behalf. Briefly this system functions as follows: in each enterprise, workers elect a certain number of representatives to the workers' council—the ultimate governing organ of the enterprise. Different committees are formed from among those elected to supervise the full-time professional managers. The powers of the workers' councils are very extensive. In consultation with communal authorities they can even appoint and dismiss the managing director of an enterprise. They also have a substantial say in investment decisions and in the disposition of surpluses.

In practice, a number of difficulties arose. Workers elected to various committees were often technically incompetent to judge the proposals made by professional management, to evaluate their performance, and to participate in strategic decisions of an enterprise. While formal authority accrued to them, they tended to act as rubber-stamping organs. Attempts have been made to educate workers and to increase their technical competence. This has caused some other difficulties. Those who succeeded in acquiring sufficient professional competence preferred to become managers rather than to retain their worker status. Another difficulty was the temptation for workers to take shorter-term views and favour distribution of surpluses among themselves rather than to make long-term investments to assure the viability of the enterprise. This was particularly true of those who were soon to retire. To offset this, the government had to impose some rules on the distribution of surpluses. Finally, the system of collective ownership and workers' self-management has been too cumbersome to apply to agriculture and would have been burdensome and unduly constraining in small-service enterprises. These reasons have contributed to the decision to restitute much of the land and small-service enterprises to private hands.

Even though ownership has been socialized in Yugoslavia, a relatively free market has been maintained. It was felt that resources could be allocated efficiently this way; a certain amount of competition between enterprises would improve their efficacy; and their autonomy would be better assured if they would have some freedom of decision as to what to produce, for whom, how, and at what prices to sell. In reality, a number of enterprises for which the initial impulses came from the government were able to develop monopoly or near-monopoly positions. Also, given the preoccupation of the political leaders to prove the economic viability of this kind of system, some inefficient enterprises were able to survive through government protection. To counter those deviations, the government tried to stimulate competition, both internal and foreign, by opening the domestic market to some imports.

A free market has an inherent propensity for cyclical variations of economic activity. Also, it permits structural and even general high unemployment. One of the ways in which Yugoslavia tackled this problem has been by exporting surplus labour to free enterprise countries. Furthermore, since this system did not seem to generate sufficient amounts of technological innovation, some foreign firms were allowed to come in on the basis of cooperation agreements and joint ventures to help accelerate technological progress and to help secure more foreign markets.

The role of government was seen as one of orchestrating economic activity by setting broad objectives, coordinating, and regulating. Since the system of governance is of the unitary power kind, the supremacy of government is taken for granted. In order to maintain workers' self-management of enterprise, however, there could be no compulsory master plans for all production and distribution units. This lack, some critics observed, led to suboptimum investments and to the favouring of regional interests. To offset this, the government had to use instruments such as differentiated interest rates on credits extended to different enterprises. It could induce the investments judged desirable by supplying generous, low-interest credits, and discourage investments considered undesirable, be it in a given sector or location, by making credits very costly and difficult to obtain.

The end purpose of market socialism is to assure workers' self-management. The rationale underlying the design of the economic system, therefore, has been sociopolitical in its character. The main pressures for changes stem from the difficulties of reconciling national interests with those of autonomous workers' collectives. There has been oscillation between central control and decentralization to permit greater local and enterprise autonomy. The key dilemma and conflicts are between what is ideologically desirable and economically efficient, between full political control and workers' self-management.

If one abstains from considerations of political and certain social costs and judges the performance of market socialism on essentially economic terms, the judgement can be fairly positive. This system has been put into place in a difficult setting. Yugoslavia is a federation consisting of different nationalities, languages, and religions. The constituent parts have had profoundly different historical experiences, such as centuries of Turkish domination over one part and of Austro-Hungarian over another. The constituent republics, therefore, aside from the differences in languages and religions, were also at different stages of economic development and of political evolution. They still vary from economically rather advanced, even sophisticated, Slovenia, to poor and backward Montenegro. Yugoslavia does not have a particularly generous natural resource base. The level of skills in the population was low. Despite these handicaps, Yugoslavia has had fairly high rates of economic growth. This was accomplished without much foreign aid, since Yugoslavia asserted its autonomy *vis-à-vis* the Soviet Union and had only a modest amount of aid from Western countries.

The willingness and the ability of Yugoslavia to export substantial amounts of its surplus labour to Western European countries has been a significant factor in its relative economic success. At times, over ten per cent of its labour force has been working abroad. This has substantially reduced the cost of unemployment and under-employment and produced a high volume of remittances from Yugoslav workers abroad, which greatly eased the balance-of-payments problems and provided the necessary foreign exchange for the import of essential goods and investment capital. It is difficult, therefore, to attribute Yugoslavia's economic survival to its particular economic system. What can be readily admitted, however, is that workers' self-management, combined with a partially free market and substantial intervention by the government, has not led to economic chaos or collapse, as wartime communism virtually did in the Soviet Union from 1918 to 1922.

CHAPTER 5

Different Roads to Common Destiny

To REACH its present state, humanity has travelled along a multitude of roads. These varied from smooth to sinuous, tortuous, and even discontinuous, with occasional sharp changes and reversals of direction. The pace has varied from painfully slow to breathtaking, as in recent decades when many changes have been compressed into a short time. Man's drives, concerns, and priorities have been changing from sheer physical survival in the battle against the forces of nature to longer-term security, to social, psychic, and intellectual satisfactions, desire to influence or dominate others.

Along the way man searched to understand the phenomena surrounding him, their origins, their purpose, and the laws they abide by, including his and other people's origins, modes of behaviour, and destinies. He yearned for prescriptions of what to do and how, to be right and successful in his pursuits or in accomplishing his fate. He united with others voluntarily or was forced into gradually bigger groups, like extended families, tribes, nations, empires. Such entities oscillated in their strength through history, sometimes breaking up or disintegrating, to decay or resuscitate to fresh strength. The reasons for bonding or being forced into bigger political entities were many: advantages of specialization, greater security, desire to explore and exploit bigger areas or new worlds. The sources of conflict have been equally numerous: differing religions, economic interests, ideologies, or competition for political power.

During this century, all of these elements have manifested themselves with greater strength. Religions have either been losing their grip or going through rapid renaissance. Technological progress has moved at unprecedented pace, helping to create great wealth, but also greater differences in wealth, and generally increasing the power of

172

man for good and evil. Some empires reached their peaks only to disintegrate rapidly. The last major war involved, directly or indirectly, virtually the whole world.

We now find ourselves with some 150 nation-states varying in size from lilliputs to supergiants at various stages of economic development, with different economic systems, with political regimes ranging from the purely autocratic to ones with broad diffusion of power and a spectrum of values, with roots in religious, ideological, or nationalistic beliefs and motives. Since countries have become more accessible and transparent to each other, the differences between them are more visible and frequently amplified by reporting—which, understandably, focuses on the extreme, the exceptional, the "newsworthy", or that which serves current propaganda purposes of some regimes. Countries are categorized into more or less homogeneous blocks according to their level of industrialization, economic interests, dominant ideology, nature of political governance, or military alliances. The world is thus carved up into mildly or sharply conflicting groupings like West–East, North–South, Industrialized, Newly Industrializing or Less Developed Countries, NATO, Warsaw Pact, or OPEC.

The United Nations, the world umbrella organization, has been an excellent body for the legitimizing of aspirations and the articulation of world concerns and priorities, but very limited in its power to resolve serious conflicts, handle the world's common problems, and develop mechanisms for effective integration of the world community.

In view of profound divisions, multiple conflicts and the relative impotence of present world institutions, is it at all realistic to talk about "common destiny" and "world order"? Is it not more appropriate to limit oneself to the analysis of the "world disorder"?*

Forces Favouring World Integration

There are powerful reasons that make it imperative for us to build up some ideas and prepare first sketches, if not the blueprints for a future world order. A number of increasingly strong forces will drive

*Bell, D., The future world disorder: the structural context of crises. *Foreign Policy*. no. 27, Summer 1977.

humanity in that direction. The most potent is the threat of total physical annihilation. The present inventory of atomic warheads would suffice to destroy the human race and, for that matter, most other living species, many times over. This destructive capacity keeps increasing. The awareness of its existence is spreading. The balance of nuclear terror is a delicate one. Normal life is not possible for prolonged periods with this threat hanging over the whole of humanity.

Physically *the world has shrunk* dramatically in the last few decades and will continue to shrink due to further developments in transportation and communication technology. It is now possible to transport virtually anthing to any point in the world within hours, whereas this used to take weeks, if not months. It is possible to hear and see events and occurrences that happen nearly anywhere on the globe. There is a growing awareness of other parts of the world and increasing identification with them. While strong animosities keep flaring up, sentiments of solidarity continue to grow, as manifested by voluntary aid to refugees or adoption of children of other races.

Economically the world is condemned also to coexistence because of the accidental scatter of natural resources and the imperatives for them to flow across national boundaries. There are only a few countries of continental size with a broad range of natural resource endowments that could opt for economic self-sufficiency, but even then at the great cost of substantially lower living standards for their populations.

Most other countries, whose patterns of production and consumption have been shaped by the cross-boundary flows of materials and goods, would collapse economically if they were suddenly cut off from others.

Technology is another element that contributes to the imperative of interdependence. In theory, any country could, with time, rediscover whatever technical knowledge already exists elsewhere. The cost of doing so and the time required, however, render such an option completely irrational. There are serious impediments to the flow of technical know-how, particularly that of direct commercial value, across national boundaries, yet the cost of acquiring what is already known in other countries is so very much smaller than discovering from scratch. Even a huge country like China has opted recently for importation of foreign technical know-how as an indispensable precondition for the success of its four modernizations.

Even *demographic trends* push us into greater interdependence. In many developing countries with already high densities, populations grow rapidly and are likely to double in the next two and a half to three decades. As the masses of children will grow to adulthood, and as birth rates will start tapering off, such countries will end up with potentially dynamic populations, with a great proportion of their people in productive ages but without sufficient opportunities for productive work. In industrialized countries, the populations are ageing, stagnating. The proportion of those who produce over those who consume has been declining and will continue to do so. In some of them, like Australia or Canada, there are still huge empty spaces and untapped resources. These factors will press both for some international migration policies and further international specialization of labour.

The Impeding Forces

There are, however, some potent restraining forces that, while they may not prevent us from ultimately converging on some world order, will certainly slow down the pace of our journey.

There are, first, the *ideological divisions*. Existing ideologies differ sharply in the prescriptions they offer for ways in which societies should be organized and governed. When it comes to economic systems, the ideological differences may be less fundamental than they appear. It has been interesting to observe how socialist countries slowly and reluctantly have rediscovered the utility of some elements of the free enterprise system, such as profitability, as a criterion in the management of enterprises, or the free market as a better allocator of some resources than the central plan. Free enterprise countries, in turn, have been searching for ways of harmonizing better the activities of privately owned enterprises and of establishing national priorities and objectives.

Among the restraining forces are *traditional conflicts* between countries with their desires to maintain their security and territorial integrity, to maintain influence zones, to ascertain the progress of their national interests, or to fulfil their imperialistic dreams. It is reassuring, however, to observe that such traditional conflicts do not always last long. Perceptions as to where the dangers for national security lie, can and do change, as do the notions of what constitutes real national interest. Empires have been broken up without much bloodshed. Most former metropolitan countries have readily reconciled themselves to the loss of empires. Many nations have turned from mortal enemies to friends, as demonstrated by current relations between the United States and Japan, or France and Germany, or the prospective new relations between China and Japan.

Religions are also among the forces restraining the progress to world unity. Religions have been among the main reasons for conflicts during the last millennia. We have known crusades, religious wars, conquests to impose the "true faith" on the "heathen" and even genocides. Naive interpretations or purposeful distortions of some articles of faith have led in the past to the extermination of fellow-men "for the love of God". Yet one finds in the same religions similar prescriptions for loving one's neighbours as oneself. It seems that man warped the intentions of his prophets rather than let himself be guided by the essence of their teachings. The current renaissance of Islam appears to be a threatening and disruptive force. The rapidity of this rebirth will undoubtedly lead to some short-term perversions. We must remember, though, that it is a religion whose adherents, after a period of glory, of cultural development and political expansion, were crushed, humiliated, relegated to secondary and subservient roles. It is natural that the new self-assertion will produce some excesses until that part of humanity which follows, in its spiritual and temporal life, the prescriptions of the Koran feels fully redeemed, secure, and self-confident.

Are There any Real Alternatives?

One can envisage alternatives to the ultimate emergence of a world order, all of which are theoretically possible but none very probable.

Total annihilation or mutual destruction of substantial parts of humanity in a global war with recourse to strategic nuclear weapons. The technical means for this exist. Sharp animosity between superpowers can provide the temptation. The likelihood of such an event is very small, however, The cost to any party involved, even to the prospective winner, would simply be too high, the damage probably beyond the recovery capacity of any country. There can be no reasoned decision to trigger off such a war. Attempts by a terrorist group or a dictator gone insane to provoke such a war would probably be "quarantined" by major powers.

Establishment of a *world empire/hegemony* by a single, powerful country. This is no longer feasible. An attempt could be made to conquer new countries one by one while blackmailing other major powers into "nonintervention" by threats of a nuclear war. Too many people have become recently independent, too many committed to the right of self-determination, to accept voluntary subjugation. The more countries will be taken over, the greater the digestion pains and the centrifugal forces. The number of people, the complexity of organizations, the resources that would be required to hold such an expanding empire by terror, would be beyond the capacity of a single nation. The empire would disintegrate before its construction could be completed.

Continuation of the present *nuclear terror balance* between the two superpowers—the United States and the Soviet Union: this is not tenable in perpetuity. First, there are several other members in the nuclear power club. With time, at least China's position in it will grow in importance, disturbing the present balance. Secondly, it seems nonsensical to be building up huge arsenals of atomic warheads at great cost without a real prospect of using them.

Complete *disintegration of the world* into fully isolated nation-states. This is economically not feasible. It would mean massive starvation in some countries, reversion to primitive modes of existence in others, and setting back of "economic clocks" by decades in the remaining ones. The populations at large would not accept such a situation for very long.

Continuation of *planetary bargain* between all nation-states and their various groupings without some universal rules, without the possibility of recourse to higher instances with arbitration and sanctioning power; such a condition is too complex and fragile to exist for a prolonged period.

Inevitability of World Order

By process of elimination we revert to a "world order" as our most probable future and, in the long run, an inevitable one. The twenty-first century should see it taking on its main contours and perhaps even a definite shape. It is likely to have among its features the following characteristics:

—Coexistence of diverse cultures, religions, beliefs, modes of existence.
—Political governance based on sharing of power without a single strong head, with permanent coalitions at all levels of governance working in a collegial fashion.
—A truly federal nature of political institutions with interlinking responsibilities and decision prerogatives at world, regional, "country", "province", county, commune, neighbourhood levels.
—A highly diffused power structure with broad participation in the decision-making processes, with more "representative" democracy working at highest levels and more "direct democracy" at lower levels of governance.
—Economic systems that would vary among regions and areas, depending on stages of economic development, population/resource ratios, and other such determinants of efficacy of economies. The systems would be designed so as to evolve as economies pass through successive stages of development, maintaining differentiation and specialization of activities, depending on climatic conditions, resource endowments, and human predispositions while tending to equalization in rewards for work and standards (not nature) of consumption.

THE NECESSARY PRECONDITIONS

There are a number of preconditions that have to be fulfilled before the world order can be ushered in. The main ones can be readily specified.

Self-determination and further diffusion of power. A multitude of nations have been recently born or reborn. There still are a number of communities with a strong sense of national identity that must also get the chance to take their fate into their own hands. While this renders world politics very complex and appears, at first sight, to take us away from a world order, it is one of the fundamental precondi- tions for its ultimate emergence. It is natural for new nation-states to relish in their new-found independence. Such nations must first be satiated by the sweet taste of full autonomy before sobering up on some of its bitternesses, before accepting the notion that the nation- state as a political entity is a phase in the existence of humanity rather than its terminal condition. The preparedness to integrate voluntarily into bigger political constructions can only come after the new or reborn nations have:

—regained their pride;
—gained confidence in their own ultimate cultural viability;
—reached a level of economic development comparable to other can-
    didate constituent states for new, bigger political constructions;
—have seen from the experience of other areas, like Western Europe,
    that it is possible to maintain full cultural autonomy, viability, and
    control over matters that affect people most closely, while being
    integrated into bigger economic and political entities.

Synchronization of stages of economic development. It would be diffi- cult to accommodate peacefully under the same political roof coun- tries at radically different stages of economic development. This is analogous to maintaining great economic inequalities within a country, which can be done either when the masses are very ignorant or by crude totalitarian means, neither of which can be a long-term reality. This synchronization is already underway with an enforced redistribution of wealth by organisms like OPEC, a substantial slow- down of most advanced countries, and accelerated development of an increasing number of newly industrializing nations.

Diffusion of wealth within countries. This is also likely to take place both for political and economic reasons. In representative democra- cies with free enterprise economic systems, this has already pro- gressed quite far. In such countries, the less wealthy (who are in the majority) form strong political constituencies and press for measures of redistribution. Also, economic development, of which the wealthier are both the main promoters and beneficiaries, cannot continue unless the bulk of the population increases its purchasing power and

180 *Road Maps to the Future*

is plugged into the market system. The process of equalization can also happen in a faster revolutionary way, as in China, where, at least, poverty has been spread equitably while preparing to do the same with wealth, which is yet to be generated.

Evolution and convergence of present societal orders. If peaceful accommodation of countries within the same world structure is to take place, their respective values must become more compatible, their political experience more similar, and their economic systems, even if remaining somewhat different, at least must not be directly opposed. Present societal orders will have to evolve in certain, desirable, directions to bring about the necessary convergence between them; these directions have been indicated and their feasibility assessed in Chapter 2, "The State of Nation-States".

The main conclusions that can be proposed are the following.

The extremes of individualistic-competitive values are not tenable in the world of shrinking spaces and resources, of complex interdependence within and between societies. The fully collectivist mode of existence does not seem sufficiently reflective of man's true nature, of his instinctive inclinations. The spread and affirmation of group-cooperative type of values is necessary and likely, this to allow man to accommodate to his fellow-men yet retain his individuality, to subordinate himself to some common purposes and higher priorities, without physical compulsion, detailed legislative regulations, or burdensome benevolent bureaucracy.

The unitary power type of governance requires imposition and cannot be sustained indefinitely in an educated society with people yearning to be subjects and not just objects. The preparedness of many people under totalitarian regimes to sacrifice privileges, physical well-being, and life itself, to assert their political rights, testifies to the above. The countervailing power type of governance leads to unnecessary polarizations, conflicts, frictions. Differences of interests, opinions, and feelings are not best resolved by choosing between "for" and "against". Political institutions have to provide means for accommodation of diverse interests. Shared-consensual type of governance provides some means of doing this without authoritarian imposition nor excessive "social entropy". It is the best option from among those humanity has experienced thus far.

Economic conditions and priorities of man change and will con- tinue to change. Consequently the systems that regulate production and distribution of wealth also need to keep evolving.

The command-state enterprise system can help a country to pass quickly through the early industrialization process, but only with significant social and political costs. It becomes unduly cumbersome in more advanced stages of economic development. An unbridled free enterprise system, in which each individual, each economic unit or sector of society pursues its own particular economic interest, does not seem able to cope sufficiently well with current problems of the less-developed or the very-advanced countries (those on the doorsteps of postindustrial stages). Some form of concerted free enterprise— which retains the dynamism of private initiative, the automatic regu- lative powers of the market place, yet which provides some means for even private property to serve the public purpose—is the model that appears most viable.

Feasibility of a World Order

The above preconditions are very demanding. One can legitimately question if they can be fulfilled. But one can also hope. Man has risen to extraordinary challenges before, when the challenge was suffi- ciently clear, the goal either attractive or indispensable, and the ways of attaining both at least discernible. During this past century, the pace of technological and commercial innovation has been excep- tionally high. Various studies repeatedly converge on the conclusion that "demand-pull" has been the main force evoking the innovative capacity of individuals, organizations, and whole nations. It is on this "demand-pull" that we have to rely to produce innovations on the philosophical and ideological fronts and, even more important, in the design of and experimentation with the required new social, poli- tical, and economic institutions.

The educational level of people is increasing everywhere. The com- munication of various phenomena that fashion our present and im- pact on our future is spreading, even if often with many distortions. The understanding by broader proportions of the population of the gaps between the old political-economic prescriptions and future needs is likely to increase, as will the awareness of the need for institutional innovation.

We have an extraordinarily rich menu of experiences behind us: wars that punish the winners, revolutions that grow perverse, of chauvinism, racism, of expansionistic, imperialistic adventures that ultimately drain the "masters", of liberation movements, a necessary step to communal adulthood. The most important factor that makes the emergence of the ultimate world order feasible is that we have in the contemporary world at least partial models of the necessary components for the construction of that order. There are countries that function well because of their people's propensity for cooperation and some voluntary subordination to societal needs; countries that have managed to integrate different linguistic communities, preserve their cultural heterogeneities, and achieve high degrees of participation of their masses in political life, high stability, and smooth functioning, essentially through an evolutionary process; countries that manifest economic prosperity, without exploited colonies, nor forceful imposition of national over individual priorities.

We also have a continent like Western Europe, which labours painfully to create a supranational structure in which there will be no master race and no slaves—clearly a useful precedent and a possible model.

Humanity will continue to travel over tortuous paths for decades to come. But they are likely to converge with time. We cannot abandon our earth. We do not wish to destroy it. No part of humanity can appropriate it. We must accommodate ourselves within its confines with some rules that will govern us all, within a single world order, our common destiny.

Measures of Effectiveness

'Seek simplicity and then mistrust it.'
(ALFRED NORTH WHITEHEAD)

There has been an explosive growth of quantification in the last few decades; tens of thousands of new standards, yardsticks, and measures have been developed to measure a multitude of phenomena. We have not, however, come up with a composite indicator of effectiveness of societies and are not likely to come up with it soon. One of the reasons is that we have not thought in terms of aggregate effectiveness of any given society, but rather only about effectiveness of particular operations, corporations, organizations, programmes, or, at best, the whole economy. We can evaluate the effectiveness of an assembly line or of an investment and, with less rigour, of programmes for reduction of unemployment, improvement of the balance of payments, or increasing of the rate of growth of gross national product. We are not yet able, though, to measure the effectiveness of a nation-state with its economic, social, or political institutions, which together determine the performance of a country.

The search is on. First to emerge were the quantitative measures of economic performance. The one measure that came into most common use and abuse has been GNP in absolute terms, on a per capita basis and, of course, its rate of growth. Nations have been ranked, classified, and judged according to GNP as an ultimate performance criterion. Even though its power remains quasi-hypnotic, the realization has spread that GNP is a measure of the volume of economic, and more specifically market, activity and not a measure of human welfare, and not even of economic welfare as such. Many goods and services are produced and valued though they are not traded on any market and thus do not get incorporated into GNP, such as household work or the upbringing of children. Other services that do get incorporated in GNP do not reflect an increase in welfare, such as various services necessitated by an increase of traffic accidents.

The limitations of GNP have evoked an interest in aggregate measures of well-being in a society, leading to such concepts as GNW (gross national welfare) or MEW (measure of economic welfare). While these were being developed, a number of separate measures of welfare emerged under the heading of social indicators, varying in clarity and precision from readily measurable daily calorific value of food intake per person to the more illusive assessment of the quality of recreational and entertainment opportunities.*

The greatest difficulty arises when it comes to measures of the effectiveness of political governance. Some objectives such as freedom and justice appear clearly desirable, but the degree of their attainment, the trade-offs involved, and the costs of attainment defy the ingenuity of statisticians.

This introduces the second main reason for the absence of composite indicators of societal effectiveness. Only a few conditions of mankind, such as an individual's life-span (life expectancy), are both readily measurable and seem to most people highly desirable. Most of the conditions of man's existence either elude precise quantification or vary enormously in the value attached to them by individuals, by communities within any given society, or by different societies.

So many factors influence the value attached to one's condition of existence—the present state of an individual, his physical and psychological make-up, his origin, social condition, his abilities, aspirations, realizations, the breadth of his horizons, the basis for comparison, reference groups and countries, the congruence between his image of an ideal societal order with his position in it, and the current reality. To a really hungry man the very next meal is of paramount importance. Radio announcements of a new agricultural policy that will improve food supply will be less important than a whisper from a friend who stole a loaf of bread and is willing to share it. To a journalist, the right to write freely is among the most important attributes of a good societal order, just as the right to profit is for a

*McHale, J. and McHale, M. C., *Basic Human Needs*, Transaction Books, New Brunswick, NJ, 1977.

businessman, or the right and the opportunity to play is for a musician. For similar reasons, and given the fact that hardly anyone's condition remains fully static, the assessments of effectiveness of societal orders vary not only between individuals, groups, communites or nations, but also over time.

Given what appear as insurmountable obstacles to the creation of an objective and universal measure of societal effectiveness, should we give up the search for them? Hardly. Firstly, assessments, evaluations, and comparisons of different societal orders are made constantly even in the absence of objective, broadly accepted criteria of effectiveness.* Making such measures and criteria more explicit would improve the ability of different societal orders to evolve, to become more effective in satisfying the needs and aspirations of the people within them.† Secondly, there are needs and aspirations that constitute an irreducible core and whose satisfaction provides some indication of how well a given society functions. Let us just mention a few: the right to be born, to exist; the right to a minimum of physical well-being; the right and opportunity to learn, think, believe, communicate, influence, love, work; the desire to matter, to make a difference.

For most such fundamental needs, we shall only have proxy measures. They will not be universal since their context will remain of paramount importance. The proxy measures will be the perceptions of the people concerned, their assessments relative to their values, needs, aspirations, and priorities. Most of the measures that we have already developed are, in fact, proxy indicators. They can be grouped, though somewhat arbitrarily, into economic, social, and political.

Economic Measures

The *total GNP* of a country does provide at least an approximate measure of its economic output and, therefore, its economic power, though not of the efficiency of the system. To have some indication of economic efficacy one has to analyse the inputs that go into the production of the output as measured by GNP. The key inputs are

---

*European olympics, *Vision*, July/August issues from 1972 through 1978.
†*Measuring the Quality of Life: Philippine Social Indicators*, Development Academy of the Philippines, 1975.

the available natural resource endowments, the existing stock of capital, the volume of investment, know-how, amount and nature of work input, and the associated costs (externalities). GNP per capita is still a reasonable indicator of the current wealth of a nation, though, of course, not of its distribution, nor the wisdom of its use nor the amount of well-being derived from it. Income distribution statistics showing the percentage of the population in various income brackets do indicate how the purchasing power is distributed, though not the sense of wealth or poverty derived from various income levels.

The annual *growth of GNP per capita* is an indicator of the increase of the man-made wealth of a country, though not of its future potential. The composition of GNP (investment, private consumption, government expenditure) is a better predictor of an economy's likely future performance, since future productive capacity is largely determined by current investment. The same is true for the sectoral distribution (primary, secondary, tertiary) of GNP. It indicates both the state of maturity of an economy and its future potential, since transfer of people from the primary to the secondary manufacturing sector invariably increases the productivity and, thus, the monetized value of the total output of an economy.

Capital output ratios, both aggregate (value of total existing capital divided by total current GNP) and marginal (new investment required, expressed as a percentage of GNP, to produce an addition of one per cent to future GNPs), are good indicators of the efficiency of investments. This, in turn, depends on the stage of economic development, resource endowment, skills of people, and the state of capital saturation.

Some indices concerning *foreign trade* also help in the assessment of a country's economic performance. Global import and export figures indicate the relative "weight" of a country in the world economy, its competitiveness, its power to influence pricing, sourcing, and the nature of goods traded. Exports and imports as a percentage of GNP, on the other hand, are indicators of the degree of dependence on the external world. The range of export products and foreign markets shows the degree of development, maturity, flexibility, and diversity, and thus of future trade security as opposed to reliance on one export commodity, the nightmare or mono-economies. The breadth of sourcing (the number of countries from which imports come) is a measure of security of future supplies. The balance of trade can be greatly influenced by natural resource endowments (e.g. having or not having oil), but it is, nevertheless, an indicator for many countries of their international competitiveness and economic effectiveness.

Balance of payments and resulting foreign reserves positions are indicators of a country's capacity to finance its imports, at least in the short-term future, and of the probable future value and solidity of its currency.

Proper assessment of economic effectiveness of a country has to include the evaluation of its future prospects. This has to take into account the available natural resources, the sustainable motivation to work, the likelihood of a constantly expanding fund of technical and organizational know-how, the existing physical infrastructure and productive facilities, the private or institutional propensity to save and invest, and the existence of an institutional infrastructure that facilitates learning, experimentation, adaptation, innovation, and generation of surpluses.

Social Indicators

Social indicators attempt to define intrinsic human needs and degrees of their satisfaction. They are labelled "social" since most human needs can only be satisfied through interaction with other human beings. Some of human needs are essentially physiological (e.g. nutrition); their satisfaction requires physical goods and services, i.e. the products of economic activity. Therefore they can be related back to some indicators of the economic effectiveness of a country. Others are more spiritual in nature, like the need of many to believe in the supernatural. The satisfaction of these needs depends on the nature of political governance, particularly in the case of freedom of religion. Other needs, such as the one to learn, which necessitates the existence of some schools, can be properly satisfied only if both the economy and political governance function well; the first providing the resources for the construction of schools and the second making political decisions to allocate such resources and shaping the nature of the educational system. In fact, the satisfaction of the needs of most people ultimately depends on the functioning of the economic system, the political governance, and the interaction between the two, both being conditioned by the values of people.

Many of the social indicators have been derived from the definition of basic human needs.* Some of them are reviewed below.

Health. There are some direct measures of health, such as infant mortality or average life expectancy, and other less-direct measures, such as the number of doctors or hospital beds per some unit of population, which are better measures of health support services than of the state of health and its enjoyment. More hospital care can reflect greater health problems or less propensity for families to take care of their sick.

Food. Measures of nutritional need are highly developed. e.g., daily calorie, protein, and vitamin requirements. Once beyond the basic intake requirements, though, we are in the realm of the unmeasurable. Food can be a great source of sensual enjoyment. Shared consumption of food has been, in most cultures and for millennia, one of the great social experiences. The importance attached to food, and the amount of satisfaction derived from it, varies enormously, heavily influencing people's perception of well-being. It is that perception that is more meaningful, though less measurable, than the calorific count.

Housing is clearly one of the universal human needs. It contributes to well-being in at least three ways: physical comfort, aesthetic pleasure, and ego satisfaction derived from a possession highly visible to others. Statistics about per-capita square metres of housing or average cost of a family house do not reflect, however, the amount of well-being derived from housing. One look at the uniformly attractive exterior of peasant houses in the Katmandu valley in Nepal probably gives a better indication of the standard of living there than either the above statistics or the per-capita income of the peasants.

Education is another area for which there are some clear measures and in which there are vast divergencies in efficacy, utilization, and valuation. We can measure the rate of literacy, average years of

*Report on the Definition and Measurement of Standards and Levels of Living, United Nations, New York, 1954.

schooling, and enrolment in schools of different age brackets. It is more difficult to assess the quality and utility of learning. How close is the match between knowledge, attitudes, skills acquired, and the opportunity for their use in gainful employment, other constructive pursuits or further spiritual development? How big are the gaps between aspirations, which are the inevitable by-products of education, and accomplishments or realizations? Are such gaps sources of pressure for greater social progress or sources of anxieties, personal frustrations, and social disruptions?

Does the educational system improve the ability of a whole nation to learn from the experience of other societies? While the above questions cannot be answered by statistics, observations across national boundaries indicate that countries vary in the degree to which they match perceived learning needs and opportunities, and their ability to learn from other socities' experience. In our era of rapid changes, learning capacity is a crucial "measure" of societal effectiveness. This has been succinctly stated as follows: "When the rate of learning is greater than the rate of change, the result is progress; when the opposite is true, the result is chaos."*

The opportunity to *work* is measured exhaustively by employment/unemployment statistics. Some conditions of work are also measurable, such as categories of jobs, hours worked per week, or accident rates. Some rewards for work, such as wages, are also measurable. Others—mainly the intrinsic satisfaction derived from doing work because of its real utility, meaningfulness, or relationships at work—are very difficult to measure. There are attitudinal surveys, but mostly we rely on negative proxy measures such as labour turnover, absenteeism, industrial unrest, or psychosomatic disorders.

Desire for enjoyable *leisure and recreation* is legitimate enough. Statistics on the number of cinemas or television sets are indicators of recreational opportunities. They may also indicate the reduced capacity or will of families to fill leisure time meaningfully, to create rather than passively to "consume" entertainment.

Social security is one of the objectives of economic development and one of its negative by-products. An old-age pension is a way to increase personal security, the sense of independence, dignity, and

*Statement by Professor R. Revans at a lecture given at the CEI, Geneva.

self-respect. Old-folks' homes, though, which often go along with old-age pensions, can be a terrible way of isolating people from their families, from normal life, from hope. The indicators of social security do not discriminate between financial independence and the psychological suffering that can be associated with it.

One can conclude the discussion of social indicators by observing that things which we can measure have real meaning only for the satisfaction of the more basic human needs. As needs evolve, their satisfaction eludes measurement, but they do not lose their meaning. The ultimate "measures" of societal health are the state of awareness of people, their sense of purposefulness, usefulness, belonging, the satisfaction with their lives' accomplishments and prospects, with that which has transpired and that which is likely.

Social needs and their satisfaction are greatly influenced by the effectiveness of the political organization. One finds, therefore, the manifestations of social well-being, or privations, reflected in the political arena.

Political Indicators

Assessment of the effectiveness of political governance is at once difficult and important, illusive and necessary, the object of great passions, and the least amenable to objective, rational analysis. In the contemporary world, with rapidly increasing numbers of educated and politically conscious people, political systems evoke more and more judgements and reactions, articulated or covert.

There is no universally accepted political model, hence we cannot come up with a set of criteria by which all types of political governance can be judged. Judgements are relative. What is perceived as good depends on what is thought to be right or just. However, it is difficult to accept the idea of each type of governance being judged on its own terms. Many human aspirations and yearnings transcend national boundaries because they stem from human nature itself. Some common yardsticks are required. But before analysing these yardsticks or indicators, we need to examine the key dimensions of political governance.

Source of power and access to it. Sources include force, demonstrated competence of those in power, or the will of the people as expressed through electoral procedures.

Principal objectives. Official and real objectives do not always coincide. They can be: to serve the interests of those in power, of some narrow sector of the population (the wealthy or the mighty), the nation as such, or the "greatest good for the greatest number".

Ways of using power. This varies from conformance to an articulated ideology, constitution, laws, announced intentions, through pragmatic adaptation to situations, to pure arbitrariness or whimsy. Partly depending on the above, the political decision-making processes can vary from transparent and predictable to opaque and even contradictory. The three main modes of using power (accomplishing the desired ends) are:

—compulsion, imposition;
—persuasion, education;
—responding to initiatives and demands.

Normally, a combination of the three modes is used, but the predominance of the first is associated with dictatorships and the last with direct democracy.

Costs of governance. These are economic costs such as the percentage of GNP absorbed by all levels of government, the number of people employed and thus unavailable for other uses, the cost of compliance with regulations, and psychic costs, such as perceived or real constraints, cumbersomeness of procedures, or the perceived omnipresence of bureaucracy.

Acceptability of power. This is the ultimate measure of perceived legitimacy, effectiveness and viability of political governance. What determines the acceptability of political institutions to the people concerned? There are a number of criteria by which people make their judgements. The priority and weight given to them vary according to prior experience, knowledge of alternatives, and, thus, currently held values and expectations in such domains as:

—freedom of: beliefs, opinions, expressions, association, mobility, opting out (emigration);
—justice, legality, fairness;
—opportunity for: education, employment, political involvement;

—efficacy of: economic performance, distributive justice, quality of life, social relations;

—external impacts, image of the country, its prestige, its perceived power.

What are the expressions, the manifestations of such judgements, which can be used as indicators of the degree of acceptability of a given government? Voter participation would appear to be the most evident yet is the most misleading. The percentage of those who participate in elections seems at times inversely proportional to the degree of freedom within a society. The more dictatorial the regime the higher the participation in elections. Frequency of voting, the range of issues on which people vote, and the choices available are somewhat better indicators.

Political opinion polls on how people judge the government or those in power are frequent in some countries (e.g., in the United States). They are better indicators of dissatisfaction than satisfaction and rarely include questions about fundamentally different political options. Worse still, they are not possible in a large number of countries.

Special attitudinal surveys, though similar to polls, are, at times, broader in scope and can be a significant measure of satisfaction or dissatisfaction with political institutions. They can measure trust or distrust of those in power, the degree of political alienation or of insecurity.* Attitudinal surveys, like opinion polls, are most common though in societies that are open and transparent and in which there is a multitude of possible manifestations of the acceptability or popularity of a government. In countries where such overt manifestations are suppressed, attitudinal surveys, even when occasionally used, are of little value.

Can we nevertheless make some assessments? Not very systematically, but it is possible. One can compare the degrees of accessibility to and participation in the political power structure and decision-making process. This is an indicator of the permeability and influenceability of a system, its flexibility, adaptability, and ability to

---

*Yankelovitch, D., Status of resentment in America, *Social Research*, **42** (4), Winter 1975.

change and evolve without violent convulsions. Among the negative measures are the oppositions of all kinds and, even more significant, the risks and costs that such oppositions imply. This varies from deprivation of the rewards that are available to those who accept the system, who are integrated into it and work on its terms, to isolation of dissidents from positions of influence, to all kinds of compulsion, and, ultimately, physical liquidation. The cost of disagreement and opposition, therefore, is a good negative proxy indicator of voluntary acceptability of any given type of political governance. One obtains a clear indication of the intensity of opposition, though not necessarily of the spread of it, when some prisoners in concentration camps, having been deprived of all other ways of self-expression and assertion, mutilate their own bodies as the ultimate way of expressing some autonomy of thought and action.

Thus the composite, though not readily measurable, indicators of overall societal effectiveness are the matches between economic endowments (natural and human) and economic accomplishments, social aspirations and social relationships, political ideals and yearnings and their fulfilment—in short, the congruence between values, needs, and their satisfaction.